AMERICAN
INDIAN
PROPHECIES

HAY HOUSE TITLES
OF RELATED INTEREST

Books

"I COME AS A BROTHER": A Remembrance of Illusions,
by Bartholomew

THE LIGHTWORKER'S WAY,
by Doreen Virtue, Ph.D.

SACRED CEREMONY,
by Steven D. Farmer, Ph.D.

A SPIRITUAL PHILOSOPHY FOR THE NEW WORLD,
by John Randolph Price

7 PATHS TO GOD, by Joan Borysenko, Ph.D.

VISIONSEEKER, by Hank Wesselman, Ph.D.

WHISPERING WINDS OF CHANGE, by Stuart Wilde

All of the above are available at your local bookstore,
or may be ordered by visiting:
Hay House USA: **www.hayhouse.com**
Hay House Australia: **www.hayhouse.com.au**
Hay House UK: **www.hayhouse.co.uk**
Hay House South Africa: **orders@psdprom.co.za**

AMERICAN INDIAN PROPHECIES

Conversations with Chasing Deer

KURT KALTREIDER, PH.D.

HAY HOUSE, INC.
Carlsbad, California
London • Sydney • Johannesburg
Vancouver • Hong Kong

Published and distributed in the United States by: Hay House, Inc., P.O. Box 5100, Carlsbad, CA 92018-5100 • *Phone:* (760) 431-7695 or (800) 654-5126 • *Fax:* (760) 431-6948 or (800) 650-5115 • www.hayhouse.com • *Published and distributed in Australia by:* Hay House Australia Pty. Ltd., 18/36 Ralph St., Alexandria NSW 2015 • *Phone:* 612-9669-4299 • *Fax:* 612-9669-4144 • www.hayhouse.com.au • *Published and distributed in the United Kingdom by:* Hay House UK, Ltd. • Unit 62, Canalot Studios • 222 Kensal Rd., London W10 5BN • *Phone:* 44-20-8962-1230 • *Fax:* 44-20-8962-1239 • www.hayhouse.co.uk • *Published and distributed in the Republic of South Africa by:* Hay House SA (Pty), Ltd., P.O. Box 990, Witkoppen 2068 • *Phone/Fax:* 2711-7012233 • orders@psdprom.co.za • *Distributed in Canada by:* Raincoast • 9050 Shaughnessy St., Vancouver, B.C. V6P 6E5 • *Phone:* (604) 323-7100 • *Fax:* (604) 323-2600

Edited by: Jill Kramer   *Designed by:* Jenny Richards

Library of Congress Cataloging-in-Publication Data

Kaltreider, Kurt.
      American Indian Prophecies : conversations with chasing deer / Kurt Kaltreider.
         p.   cm.
      ISBN 1-56170-497-0
      1. Indian philosophy—North America. 2. Indians of North America— Religion.   I. Title.
      E98.P5K35   1998
      299'.7—dc21   98-19217
                                                                          CIP

ISBN 1-56170-497-0

07 06 05 04   9 8 7 6
1st printing, September 1998
6th printing, October 2004

Printed in the United States of America

To Grandmother Samuel Ella Iona Wood,
the last full-blooded Indian in my line.
To my Grandfather Ernest Brannock—
I think I got the message, Pop.
To my mother Lenna Brannock Kaltreider,
and my father D. Frank Kaltreider, M.D.
Thank you for your love.

And, last, to the American Indian Elders.
Mitakuye Oyasin.

CONTENTS

Foreword by Lewis Mehl-Madrona, M.D., Ph.D.. viii
Acknowledgments xi
Introduction: *A Personal Note from the Author* xiii

CHAPTER ONE
The Call. 1

CHAPTER TWO
The Meeting. 13

CHAPTER THREE
Dreams and Prophecies 19

CHAPTER FOUR
The American Indian Holocaust. 39

CHAPTER FIVE
Prophecies of Coming Times 79

CHAPTER SIX
Spirituality and a New Integral Culture 117

CHAPTER SEVEN
Values: Teach the Children Well. 147

CHAPTER EIGHT
The Wisdom of the Elders: Community and Happiness . . . 167

CHAPTER NINE
Healing the Body and the Planet 187

Notes 209
About the Author 217

My friend,
They will return again.
All over the Earth,
They are returning again.
Ancient teachings of the Earth,
Ancient songs of the Earth,
They are returning again.

My friend, they are returning.
I give them to you,
And through them
You will understand,
You will see.
They are returning again
Upon the Earth.

— song of His Crazy Horse,
Lakota Warrior and Prophet

FOREWORD

When Chasing Deer was sufficiently old to see more of sunset than sunrise, he sought the right person to receive his wisdom. While wisdom cannot be bought or sold, neither can it be kept close to the chest, hidden under a barrel, or stashed under a buffalo rug. Unshared wisdom festers, decays, and disintegrates if not passed to future generations. Are you worthy of the wisdom of Chasing Deer? Are you ready to receive the burden of his knowledge? For knowledge must lead to action.

I was told that Kurt Kaltreider had written a book about Chasing Deer, but that was not so, since Chasing Deer had found Kurt and planted this wisdom in his sleeping mind. Kurt fought Chasing Deer at every step of this writing, which is how I know it to be authentic. Perhaps Chasing Deer dreamt Kurt and enrolled him to pass on this wisdom to you. Chasing Deer tortured Kurt until these words had to emerge, had to enter the world, had to shine forth like precious turquoise and silver.

Kurt has honored us and all of our ancestors by allowing Chasing Deer to write this book through him, to flow through his veins, to disseminate the wisdom of Native American people, to become a living prophecy, and to share a worldview that reflects sun and sky, earth and water. Why would Chasing Deer want to do this, and why would Kurt help him? Because culture is breaking apart, and families are splintering. Because the values that make humans transcend greed are woefully absent. Because prophecy is needed more now than ever before in history as we stand on the brink of destruction of the human race, comforted only by the knowledge that the Earth can survive without us. "The place where the roots have been pulled out leaves a wound, a raw and empty place that I feel like a gnaw in my belly." The words of this book can fill those empty places in you.

The day Kurt's book arrived was the day that Franny, one of my patients, introduced me to walking meditation through the nearby cemetery, an ironic juxtaposition. I would have never walked there alone, fearing death, fearing loneliness, fearing emptiness. Franny gave me permission to be there, her bald head shining in the sunlight, so aware of her potential mortality. She carried a gentle wisdom as we very slowly and mindfully walked through that cemetery, the juxtaposition of life and death before us, her bald head a symbol of the struggle with cancer, of her radiation therapy, of life and death distilled into a few short glances.

American Indian Prophecies provides a similar experience as it interweaves the compassionate and loving teachings of Chasing Deer with the stark facts of the Native American holocaust (over 100 million perished). As Kurt describes Chasing Deer's craggy face, I see his own. Like Chasing Deer, Kurt's loving kindness and good humor perpetually dance across his eyes. Like Chasing Deer, Kurt's long gray hair also falls free over his old plaid shirts. Like Chasing Deer, when I met Kurt, he was laughing.

Kurt's humor makes the shocking passages bearable. They happened—he cannot ignore them. This book has taught me facts about our ancestors that I did not know. But it does not dwell in the victim mode. It looks ahead to a future. Even if a future is not possible according to some prophecies.

Despite Chasing Deer's admonition to bear with a long-winded man, the material flows rapidly and smoothly. Through Chasing Deer, we learn about the life and moral character of the First Americans. We learn how European invaders portrayed us as savages to justify conquest, to make us less than human and, therefore, beneath God's laws. We learn that Europeans were initially greeted with great kindness and hospitality. The first-hand accounts are well referenced, convincing, yet not overly scholarly. Consider Columbus, who wrote, "Of anything they have, if you ask them for it, they never say no; rather they invite the person to share it, and show as much love as if they were giving their hearts. . . . "

Kurt and I share the desire to preserve and protect Native American religion. His stories of religious persecution as early as 1629 are enlightening. We encounter the cycle of abuse, as the previously persecuted Puritans persecute the Native people in turn. How tired we are of the ongoing attempt to convert us to Christianity. Even today, on reservations, a major threat to Native American spirituality is fundamentalist Christianity and its continued mission to eradicate our way of worship. The fight for spiritual survival continues in 1998 as it did in 1629.

Kurt does not have the answers for why these atrocities happened—none of us do—although he raises some important possibilities. People were meant to live tribally. Tribal life encourages sharing and cooperation, unlike the large communities we now find. Our hierarchical, almost military, society actually spawns values of competition and violence. Hurting anonymous people is so much easier than hurting your neighbor, on whom you must rely for help and sustenance.

Kurt's message is also revealed in the prophecies. Bad times are coming, but also miraculous times, yet survival requires change; it requires community. Community prevents murder and the myriad social problems we see in the inner cities. Prophecy points toward community. People are changing fast, and Native American philosophy and wisdom can guide them on their path to greater wholeness.

Throughout Native American prophecy and wisdom, we return to the need "to live in harmony in smaller groups once again, with all the generations present and committed to a higher purpose," the essence of His Crazy Horse's vision of how the future could be survived. The future must be built on relationships, not economics, at least not profit-driven economics. For all cannot profit; some must suffer. Nowhere is this more obvious than in my field of health care, where big business has taken hold and profits motivate most clinical care decisions. There are islands of hope, however.

At the University of Pittsburgh Medical Center Shadyside, where I work, we are helping to create a small tribe of complementary medicine within the larger institution. As the Medical Director of our Center for Complementary Medicine, I am encouraging our practitioners to look to Native American wisdom and prophecy as our inspiration for how to treat patients. In my book *Coyote Medicine,* I describe what I learned from Native American healers that all health practitioners should embody. We are working to practice in this way.

While we are far from perfect and still struggle to practice our values within an institutional setting, I hope His Crazy Horse would smile upon our efforts as he rides on the wings of an eagle overhead.

And I hope Kurt's book can inspire each of you to learn these values and practice them, creating your own small, sustainable tribes so that we can all benefit, and someday come together as we share in the global powwow.

— Lewis E. Mehl-Madrona, M.D., Ph.D.
Medical Director, Center for Complementary Medicine
Faculty/Residence Programs • UPMC Shadyside, Pittsburgh, PA

ACKNOWLEDGMENTS

This book was only written because of the support and encouragement given me by Reid Tracy, president of Hay House. Thank you, Reid, for the opportunity to put my heart into print.

I want to thank the following for their scholarship and insight: Vine Deloria, Jr., for his fine book *God Is Red*; Steven McFadden, for his *Profiles in Wisdom*, especially the record of his conversations with Grandfather Commanda (as I had difficulty remembering all that Grandfather told me when I visited him at the reserve); the historians David E. Stannard, Richard Drinnon, Francis Jennings, James Axtell, and Thomas and Carol Christensen, upon whose research I relied heavily. No student wishing to know the true history of the Americas should be without their books.

To my many friends both in the Native community and outside of it, I thank you for your patience and understanding, especially Alan Shackelford, M.D., whose part Choctaw and Cherokee ancestry was a delight to discover; David Hibbard, M.D.; Lakota Cant'e (Dik Darnell); and the Cherokee/Lakota Lewis Mehl-Madrona, M.D., Ph.D.

I want to give a special thanks to Sonny and Dik, who have helped me with my vision. I salute both of you with our mutual special reverence for the life of the late Ceremonial Chief and medicine man Frank Fools Crow. *Lela pilamayan.*

Without the extensive editorial assistance and experienced hand of Joan Borysenko, Ph.D., this book would not have come alive. I am also grateful for the excellent suggestions of Jill Kramer, my editor at Hay House; and to Christy Salinas, for the beautiful cover design.

And last, thanks to the spirits of Minnetoska and Whitethorn, to Grandfather Hemlock and all the campers from whom I learned what true community and hence, life, is all about. See you at the reunion!

INTRODUCTION
A PERSONAL NOTE FROM THE AUTHOR

Unlike so many children of mixed blood heritage, I knew that I was part Indian for as long as I can remember. It was never hidden from me. Even if it had been, I had only to look into the ancient eyes of my grandfather's rugged face to see both a wisdom and a sadness that was clearly not of the dominant culture in which I spent my childhood years. There was also something telling about the high, prominent cheekbones and somewhat tawny color of my grandmother and her sister. They were both incredibly strong and beautiful women. There was a fearlessness and independence about them uncommon for the age into which they were born. I don't know why my grandfather and I spent so many Sundays alone in his room when I was a child. I can seldom remember either my older sister or younger brother being there. I would quietly sit while Pop, as we called him, told me stories from history or read me poetry. I cherished our time together. There was something in his soul that reached out to me in a way that no other did. It was as if there was some ancient wisdom he wished to impart to me. Yet, I could sense a reluctance, as if he did not want to disturb my comfortable life.

At times, Grandfather shared the struggles of his own life. When times were tough for him as a young man, he would go to county fairs and take on all comers in the boxing ring to help support himself. I could imagine the rednecks in Dorchester County, Maryland, just itching to have a shot at the "breed." But Pop never lost a fight. He was built like a bulldog. Yet it was hard for me to imagine this gentle man flooring one man after another. I knew only the softness of his hand, the sweetness of his smile.

When Pop died in 1964, I stood over his lifeless body wondering what stories had died with him. My mother's side of the family were early settlers on the Eastern Shore of Maryland. They lived in the area of the Choptank and Nanticoke rivers named for two of the Indian tribes who once populated the surrounding area. In the early 1700s, Queen Anne of England granted much of what is now the Eastern Shore of Maryland to my ancestor Lord Hurley for "services rendered to the Crown." I don't know the story of what became of those ancestors, but by the late 1800s, my relatively land-poor great-grandfather married a Nanticoke Indian. She had the curious name of Samuel Ella Iona Wood. She was my grandfather's mother.

From the time I was old enough to go off by myself, I spent as many hours as possible in the woods. Then as now, nature was where I felt safe, alive, happy, and at home, although I was raised in the teeming city of Baltimore. As a child, I despised city life— the filth, the pavement, the smokestacks, and the crowded conditions. The dislike was deep and visceral. From the time I was six years old, my parents and grandfather gave me a gift of summers in the wilderness that turned out to be the most precious and meaningful foundation of my life.

About the third week of every June, every summer for the next 13 years, I boarded the train headed for the pristine mountains of Western Maryland and West Virginia. At the relatively primitive summer camp, I was free, surrounded by old-growth forest barely touched by the rapacious hand of "civilized" man.

Each day was filled with swimming in the cold lake, riding horses, archery, crafts, hiking in the seemingly endless mountains, and learning about the plants and animals with whom we shared that wonderful refuge.

We lived in perfect equality—each camper came with only one trunk and one duffel bag, with each receiving the same small allowance from which we could buy supplies such as toothbrushes and candy. We all shared in the chores of keeping our respective cabins neat and clean, and each cabin functioned as a clan. We ate together, played together, and sat together at our meals and at the council fire. We were inseparable.

There were no complaints about the lack of electricity, hot water, or heat. Bathing in the cold lake and drinking from the streams seemed perfectly natural. Children came from all walks of life, rich and poor, yet no comparisons were made.

In 1980, when I was in my mid-30s, one of the former campers named John organized what has come to be an annual reunion every September for those of us who shared most of our childhood summers together. We were amazed that the bonding of our youth had not waned with the passing of the years and the growing responsibilities of adulthood. There were heartfelt hugs and tears as we all gathered together at camp the September of our first reunion. It was as if by John's determination a great Diaspora had come to an end and the clan was reunited. We have been gathering every September since for the past 18 years, coming literally from the four corners of the United States.

We almost never talk of occupations, money, possessions, or accomplishments. All any of us seem to desire is the presence of the others and to share our old camp songs, laughter, and the council fire. Emotionally, it seems that for all of us, time has stood still, for we have a bond that neither time nor circumstance can break. In the 18 years that we have gathered, I have missed only a few reunions, something I hope will never happen again for as long as I live.

Last year John was the first old camper to pass over to the spirit world, and many of us came to say farewell. The last person I hugged good-bye on the day of the funeral was a man I had known from the time I was six years old. He is a successful businessman, a bit burly and a true mainstream American. As we hugged, I felt a stream of moisture gliding down my cheek, and when I looked into my friend's face, I could see that he was crying. When our eyes met, he said, "Please never miss another reunion. When one of us is missing, the body is not complete, and deep inside we mourn."

Over the years, I have returned to camp frequently for periods of solitude and reflection. Almost immediately I hike to one of the many streams where an ancient hemlock tree grows. The base of the tree is curved in such a way that it welcomes your back and invites you to rest. I have gone to that tree hundreds of times over the past 50 years or so. There I think, or more important, feel and meditate. In the arms of Grandfather Hemlock, there is a deep peace and sense of connection to the Earth.

I have since discovered that nearly all the campers went to that same tree for the same nourishment. At first I felt a little bit robbed of what seemed a special relationship, and then I realized that the tree was not only a personal friend, but a tribal friend that comforted and spoke to us. I felt ashamed for my initial self-centered response, and now when I go to Grandfather Hemlock, I pray for all of us.

Camp was started in 1927 by Pop and Mom Hansen. Pop Hansen was a schoolteacher, and where he got the money to buy such an expanse of acreage and build a camp has always been a mystery. But he loved and respected the land and somehow managed to call it into his care. He used natural and native products in constructing the cabins, aiming for minimal alteration of the environment. The lake bore an Indian name for peace, and the cabins represented various Indian Nations.

When Pop was getting on in years, he sought out just the

right person to pass the camp on to. Money was not a factor—only the goodness of the person and their intention to steward the land and care for the children in the summers. Pop found Chester Johns, a Polish immigrant and shop teacher in the public schools of Baltimore. He was hardly a man with resources to buy a thousand-acre camp and run it. And since the camp made no money, it was truly a labor of love.

When ill health befell Ches, he, too, sought out just the right person to take over the camp. It took two years before he found a schoolteacher from Ohio. Throughout all the years of the reunions, many of us grew to love this man, also—but not all of us. Many of the women warned that his heart was not in the right place. We men thought that they must be wrong. Unfortunately, they were not. Ultimately, this man used the camp for his own financial gain. Like his predecessors, the time came to pass it on, but he had no intention of finding "just the right person." It was to go to the highest bidder for development.

The campers gathered, talked by phone, and wrote to one another. We hired an appraiser and offered to buy the camp for an amount well above the appraisal price. But the betrayer, as many of us think of him, would not be moved. The camp was to be sold off in parcels to the highest bidders, and most of us did not want to buy, adding wealth to his coffers. Fortunately, some ten years earlier, several campers had bought the Lone Wolf property contiguous to camp. This is where we now meet every September.

Not long after the decision was made to develop the land, one of the old campers named Kathy went on a business trip to San Antonio. There she met a psychic to whom she revealed nothing but her name. Kathy was told that she was in mourning because her sacred land was being taken. The land, she was informed, was once a gathering place for many tribes. It had been a place of peace, ceremony, and trading where many different tribes had gathered for centuries.

Kathy sat dumbfounded, but remained silent. What the psychic told her next brought her to tears. In this lifetime she had shared that land with many of the Indians from that long-forgotten time, and the bond they shared was of enormous strength. One day, the psychic prophesied, the land would revert to its original state, and the time of sorrow would end.

The following September, Kathy and I drove to camp together. Along the dirt road about a mile from camp, we passed a historical marker that had not been there before. In fact, for the more than 40 years we had driven and walked that road, there had never been a sign of any sort. I asked Kathy to back up. The sign read: Site of THE GREAT WARRIOR PATH. SHAWNEE, DELAWARE, MINGO, ALGONQUIN & OTHER GREAT TRIBES USED THIS TRAIL BEFORE THE AREA WAS SETTLED.

We looked at each other in amazement. The path went right by Grandfather Hemlock and the site of our council fire, which was most sacred to us all. Later that week I was eating breakfast in town. I asked the old mountain man next to me if he knew the betrayer who had sold our camp for development. "Yes," he said, "he has been in very poor health and has gained so much weight that he can hardly get around. Old Indian curse for selling that land!"

All my life I have seemed to move uneasily between two cultures. The son of an academic physician and a nurse, I sought higher education and received a doctorate in philosophy from the University of Tennessee. Based on a mathematical formulation derived from my field of formal axiology, or the mathematics of value, I developed a highly successful and acclaimed system of investment research. And yet I have never been comfortable in that world. My Indian ancestors have continued to call to me.

Yet, I had little to return to in my Nanticoke heritage. Since the tribe was on the Eastern Shore of the United States, it was one of the first to be wiped out by the European settlers. My people intermarried with Black slaves, so at powwows today, we are indeed a mixed group. Some appear distinctly black or white,

others Indian, and many an exotic mix. Few of our original ceremonies remain, and the last person to speak the language died in
1859. Yet our annual powwow continues to grow and is now one
of the largest in the United States.

As is typical for the federal government, which wants Indians
to assimilate and lose their cultural identity, the Nanticoke tribe
has no official recognition. We are fighting this in the courts.
Consequently, even the few full-bloods left are not allowed to
claim their proper ethnic and cultural identity. I have personally
found Lakota teachers to tutor me in the ways of indigenous
Americans and have a deep commitment to keeping the old ways
alive and of protecting Grandmother Earth.

The old Grandfather Willow Tree that you will meet in this
book is drawn from my own experience with Grandfather
Hemlock. Nature speaks to us, teaches us the lesson that all life is
sacred, and tells us that what we do to the Earth we do to ourselves. The prophecies you will read about in this book call to
mind the words that the psychic uttered to my friend Kathy. The
land will be restored again to its sacred state. It is my fervent hope
that this will happen as the good hearts of people are awakened to
the fact that the Earth is a living being in which we continue to
evolve. If we damage her, we will change the course of our own
evolution and become mutants—isolated, violent, and unhappy.

We are at a crossroads now. The Earth has been damaged
almost beyond repair, and despite the material comforts that
Americans have achieved, many of us are depressed and anxious.
The ancient prophecies of many American Indian tribes say that
we are about to enter a time of Purification when life as we know
it will be destroyed as the Earth tries to come back into balance.
Yet there is a blueprint for healing, for living in right relationship
with one another and with nature that is the gift and legacy of the
American Indian.

In this book, through a series of conversations with two fictional characters—an old Lakota Elder named Chasing Deer; and

a young, privileged white student named John—the choice between Purification and a New Dawn in our culture is made clear. As a former philosophy professor and academic, I have researched the history and underlying assumptions of American Indian and Western culture. I have studied the American Indian holocaust and the stunning prophecies of the destruction of the American Indian—and I've studied the renewal of this culture, which is, thankfully, beginning to take place.

As you read the conversations between John and Chasing Deer, you might recognize the two voices, the two cultures, that meet in my own blood. Although the encounter between the two men is fictional, the material on which it is based was carefully researched. In the Notes section, you will find many interesting books and articles that can lead you much further into the heart and mind of a noble and remarkable culture.

If that culture is to be preserved, then the elders and medicine carriers who have carried on its traditions through 500 years of oppression and destruction need our support. To that end, one-half of all the royalties from this book will be donated to a non-profit foundation, The Native American Cultural Preservation Fund. Should you find it in your heart to help, your donation would be greatly appreciated by the traditional peoples of this land. Their ancient traditions may, in fact, be the salvation of us all. Please send your tax-deductible contributions to:

The Native American Cultural Preservation Fund
393 Dixon Road
Boulder, CO 80302

CHAPTER ONE

THE CALL

As we grow older, we develop the gift of retrospection. Rising above the tapestry of our life, we can look down upon the byways we have traveled. There are inevitably places where the road grows small, or dead-ends, and we have to search for a new route. Some of these changes in direction are gentle, subtle. Others are earthshaking. The ground rumbles beneath our feet, and we experience an upheaval that changes both the inner and outer landscape drastically and irrevocably. Such a radical transformation erupted in the life of John Stewart Pearson, called like a wild thing to his willing heart, during the summer between graduating from Dartmouth College and beginning Harvard Law School.

At 22, John was a tall, well-muscled young man with steady blue eyes and a thick shock of sandy blond hair that fell forward, though cropped rather short. He often smoothed it back off his high forehead with surprisingly long, delicate fingers. A square jaw and a patrician nose gave his pleasant face a pensive, serious look. He carried himself a bit stiffly, as if some internal censor were busily taking notes on his posture for report to some higher authority.

Were it not for a quick smile that brought a mischievous light to his azure eyes, revealing a puckish gap between his two front teeth, John might have looked bookish. Even his dungarees were neatly pressed, falling over a pair of shiny loafers at precisely the right length for dress trousers. A light blue button-down shirt completed his typical uniform, unremarkable except for one oddity. A thick brown belt of handworked leather, closed with a heavy buckle of antique silver and turquoise, provided a strange counterpart to an otherwise conservative look.

The belt was a gift from his college roommate, Tommy Chasing Deer, who had attended Dartmouth on scholarship as part of the school's Native American program. From their first meeting, the two had recognized a strange kinship despite their singularly different backgrounds. Tommy had grown up near Rapid City, South Dakota, on the Pine Ridge Reservation where the once-proud remnant of the Oglala Lakota Nation was herded up and penned in after their final defeat. He was lean and lanky, his own dungarees unpressed and falling over perpetually scuffed and dusty cowboy boots. Thick black hair, eyes like dark forest pools, a ruddy complexion, and high cheekbones gave Tommy a rugged, handsome look. Like John, he had finished near the top of his class. Tommy was on his way back to Pine Ridge to resume an apprenticeship with a medicine carrier who had begun training him in his early teens, and who continued that training over the summers and breaks between classes.

Tommy had been raised in the traditional ways of his people, and he had a deep commitment to protecting and teaching those ways, while bringing in whatever Western knowledge would benefit his people without compromising their values of respect for one another and for the Earth. Tommy's great-grandfather, Chasing Deer, from whom he had adopted his surname, also benefited from his grandson's foray into Western culture. The old man was a keeper of archives, of the ancient prophecies of all Native Americans, including the Lakota (or Sioux) Nation. To help bring a better future into existence, he always said, one had to remember the past and learn from it. To that end, Chasing Deer archived not only the past, but also the medicine, politics, philosophy, and social trends of modern times. Tommy fed him a steady stream of books and articles so that he could better serve his people.

John, too, sought to serve his people—the rather abstract group that he thought of as The American Public. He was headed along the same road that most of the men in his family had traveled for the better part of three centuries: a life in law and politics. In the naivete and nobility of youth, he had imagined his family's long-term involvement in the power structures that run the United States government as public service. But as he stood ready to follow in their footsteps, doubts had begun to dog him. How much had his forebears been motivated by public service, and how much by a self-serving interest in maintaining their own wealth and power? Was the American Dream and the emphasis on materialism what he wanted to support? Where, truly, did his heart lie?

From the birth of this nation, John could count no less than ten senators, twelve congressmen, five ambassadors, and four secretaries of state that bore his family name; and at least one man in every generation had been a presidential advisor of some note. They were among America's landed gentry, an elite group that wields far more power than the average citizen of the world's largest democracy could begin to comprehend.

John's mother, Margaret Briarley Pearson, was from an old Virginia family that had managed to keep its wealth intact through The War Between the States, as any real Southerner calls the Civil War. The land she inherited from her father had been in their family since the late 1600s, and to their credit, it was largely untouched—other than the clearing of fields from the days when tobacco had added to the family's fortune. By the time John was born, the Briarley Plantation was a horse farm upon which his grandparents raised prize Arabian horses. John's family, his parents, and his sister Little Margaret had spent part of the summer months there throughout all of his childhood. It was a place where both his imagination and his body could roam free.

Brooks and streams ran through stands of old-growth forest

at Briarley. The fragrance of wild jasmine was like a tonic for nerves stretched taut by the frantic pace of the world outside. The nearly two thousand acres of rolling hills and shady dells recalled a more peaceful and leisurely time when one's senses could spread out and open like a flower, rather than recoiling in fear and self-protection. At Briarley another part of John seemed to emerge, as if he were stepping out from behind a mask or taking off a pair of too-tight shoes. As he frequently told Tommy, "There's something magical about that land and my relationship to it—it's as if I can expand there and fill my own skin."

After graduation, John and Tommy went to Briarley together for a two-week vacation before Tommy returned to the reservation and John set out on a European tour—his graduation present. The two frequently went to John's special spot, a place that he had discovered in his childhood and that drew him like a magnet. It was a giant willow tree, its trunk at least four feet in diameter, that arched gracefully over a good-sized stream, deep enough to jump into by swinging out over the water on a knotted rope that hung from one of the willow's thick branches. The banks of the stream were lined by a sentinel of stately willows whose pink roots floated in the current like water spirits.

There, on a large, flat rock beneath the oldest and grandest tree, Tommy and John sat companionably in silence. John picked up a willow branch, torn from its place by the wind, and began to slowly strip off the leaves, throwing them into the stream to be carried away by the insistent current. "Sometimes I feel so lost, Tommy, and so confused. Who wouldn't be grateful to have the opportunities that I do—the education, the money, the connections, the chance to help our country? But most of the time, I feel an ache inside, a kind of tender, lonely place. This is the only place I feel really peaceful. The rest of the time I feel like a ball of tumbleweed, blown wherever the chance for advancing academically and professionally lead me. Maybe I should give up on law school and raise horses."

Tommy was quiet for a long time, letting John's thoughts and feelings find their place inside him. "Johnny-O," he called his friend by the kind of secret name bestowed on those we love, "I know how much this land is a part of your soul. It gives you roots, a sense of place and history, and also a way to be with your people. Here I sense you shifting into a whole other part of yourself, like you're becoming resonant with the land and it's teaching you, calling you to your highest vision. Maybe that's the source of your dilemma. You feel whole here, and fragmented in the outer world. I feel the same way about my own sacred land. In the Black Hills, I come more fully alive. And yet my destiny called me away for years of education. But maybe we're the lucky ones. We can feel the difference between being rooted and rootless."

John pulled his long legs to his chest and rested his head on them, eyes closed, the reflections of the sun in the water painting ribbons of light across his thoughtful features. "We're such a mobile culture, Tommy. Parents and kids living in different cities, families broken apart. Everyone scrambling for a buck to buy a better car or a new television. And worse still, we call this rootlessness freedom, the American Dream. The place where the roots have been pulled out leaves a wound, a raw and empty place that I feel like a knot in my belly." John sat in silent reflection as they both felt inward for that spot.

"I think every human being is pretty much the same, Tommy." John looked up and sought his friend's eyes. "We want to be happy. So, as a culture, we've tried to fill that empty place with stuff like clothes and cars, televisions and stereos, drugs, alcohol, money, sex, entertainment, power, travel. We call it the 'good life,' and if I move into public service and follow my family road, that's what I'll be serving. Isn't there another way, Tommy? Some way to heal that rootlessness, that lost feeling? Some way for people to find home? If there is, then that's what I want to serve."

John was quiet for a moment as his words vanished with a

warm breath of wind. "But I don't know how," he finished softly.

Tommy chuckled, an unexpected dimple creasing his left cheek. "Hau, brother, you're so serious. Lighten up, and then maybe some insights will come. Remember how Kekûlé discovered the structure of the benzene ring by dreaming of a snake with its tail in its mouth? You've asked the most important question, 'How shall I serve?' with good heart, good intention. Now you have to let The Great Mysterious, the voices of the Spirit World, speak to you and guide you."

Tommy got up and brushed crumbled leaves from his pants, holding a hand out to help John up. "But first, how about a game of tennis? I'll beat your butt and wear you out. Then you can come back here, to your special place under Grandfather Willow, and think. In my culture, we would say this is sacred land for you, and that it can teach you and guide you on a good road."

The dream came not after tennis, but the following morning after John's stomach was filled with a hearty Southern breakfast, mustered up by Jessie, the family cook and confessor to little boys and girls. Jessie was like a second mother to John, and her food was enriched with her love for him.

She'd raided the henhouse at dawn and brought back a dozen little brown eggs from the Bantam chickens who were descendants of the ones John had carried everywhere, tucked under his arm, as a child. Smithfield ham, bacon, homemade grits, lavishly buttered toast, an assortment of her own jams, a little fish roe, and, of course, red-eye gravy completed the menu. After breakfast, Tommy settled into the old string hammock in the peach orchard to read, and John sought the guidance of Grandfather Willow as his friend had suggested.

Settling into a hollow in the tree's massive trunk, John felt a kind of bittersweet melancholy. Gratitude for the beauty surrounding him and for all the gifts he had been given in this life welled like an ache in his chest. Yet he felt pulled by the power of his longing to serve, to take a road different from the rest of his family. He felt like praying, but as a fallen-away Episcopalian, he was unsure of how to do it, or even who or what he might be praying to. God as the old bearded guy in the sky held no appeal. Surely the Creator was beyond gender, beyond any physical form or capacity of the human mind to imagine. *Perhaps,* he thought, *that's why Tommy's people referred to the Creator as The Great Mysterious.*

As he pondered these questions in the silence woven from birdsong and breeze, John felt himself relax more deeply into the tree's embrace. It was as if he wanted to be one with the tree—to see what it had seen, to feel what it had felt as it had silently watched the march of time beneath its limbs. The Earth around him seemed to be teeming with life in a way that he had not experienced before, and a strange but peaceful energy emanated from its heart. He touched the ground and began to pray.

It wasn't long before John's head began to nod, and he found himself in that twilight zone between sleep and wakefulness where the two worlds touch. Even while part of his senses were aware of the tree at his back and the call of the mourning doves in its branches, another part of himself rose up, as free as a bird, and he found himself atop the tree, observing what appeared to be an Indian village. Although this state of being was entirely new to John, he didn't question whether he was asleep or awake. It didn't matter. He had the deepest sense that whatever he was seeing was realer than real.

Far below, a group of young Indian boys were playing a spirited game that was like a combination of tag and hide and seek. Their laughter rippled on the breezes and touched the place of his longing. They were happy. The women of the village were busy either tending the luxuriant fields of vegetables or sitting outside their small homes made of branches and thatch, preparing vegetables for storage. They carried their babies on their backs and stopped frequently to nurse them. The sense of joy with which they worked and mothered sent shivers through John's body. There was no feeling of drudgery or boredom. All he could think was that their lives were a form of praise, a prayer of thanksgiving to the Creator.

The women chattered good-naturedly and often broke out into a laughter so hearty that John strained to hear what they were saying. But the ribbons of speech that fluttered to him were in a completely foreign tongue. Every now and then, some children would leave the game they were playing, run to where the women were, and grab something to eat, darting back to the game as quickly as silverfish. There were few adult males to be seen, except for a number of very old ones, a number John took to be far out of proportion to the size of the village.

He wondered how there could be so many old ones in a time when people were supposed to die young from infectious disease and poor nutrition. The elders, too, were busy, working flint and other stones into arrowheads and various tools. The strength and ease with which they worked belied their advanced years. And as with the women and children, their laughter was infectious.

In a clearing just outside the village, a man as ancient as the stones was instructing a small number of young men who sat around in a circle, nodding solemnly as he spoke. John wondered if he were a chief or medicine man, as the young adults clearly held him in the greatest respect and reverence. They concentrated intently on his every word, waiting for a signal before speaking. Every so often the old man would gesture with a wave of his hand, and the young men would ask questions.

Suddenly the old man began to gesture at John. It took a moment to realize that the elder had seen him and was actually calling him down from the tree. With surprising nimbleness, John climbed down from his perch in the willow's high branches and began to approach the circle. He could feel his heart fluttering against his rib cage like a captured bird, and his mouth went dry. He didn't know what to say or do, and was afraid of being disrespectful, although he had no fear of harm. Later that day, John entered this account of his dream into his journal.

The old Indian nodded to me, and the young men shifted to give me a place in the circle. I thought to myself, *What am I going to do? How will we understand one another since I can't speak their language?* So I sat in silence and tried to understand them with my other senses.

The old man was bare-chested, since it was so hot, and was dressed as they all were, in leather leggings. On his breast lay a strange totem, the foot of a bird. He began to sing a haunting melody as he held up an ornately beaded pipe, with an eagle feather hanging from its stem. He offered a pinch of tobacco to the four directions, to the four winds, the Grandmother Earth and The Great Mysterious, loading the pipe with special prayers for each direction.

As he finished the ceremonial act, I felt the strangest sensation. It was as if everything dissolved into light, while still retaining form, and whatever question was in my mind was instantly answered. The presence of wisdom carried with it an awesome sense of love, as if creation itself were spun from a loving light. I asked why I was here, and I knew—in the deepest part of my being—that this was my destiny and my path to service.

The men began to pray in their tongue, and remarkably, I understood them as well as if they had spoken English—better, in fact, for I understood the intentions of their hearts, and I felt how their prayers built a bridge between the past and the future.

One man prayed for his people, enumerating the illnesses, the betrayals, and the killings that he knew would soon wipe out his tribe as the European settlers drove them from their lands.

Another prayed for the European invaders, seeing over 500 years into the future, to my time. He spoke of strange wonders, unknown to their world. Of shiny-colored boxes that traveled on wheels, of talking boxes with pictures, of metal birds that roared, of poisoned rivers and black vapors that choked the lungs, and of a sad people who had lost their hearts and their sense of connection with one another and the Earth. He called the Spirits to serve those people, to return them to a good road and give them happy hearts again.

A third man prayed for the children—for his own children and those of his tribe, and for the children of the future whom he saw being killed by other children and even by their parents.

A fourth man prayed for Grandmother Earth, who he said would soon be raped and plundered as men sought to dig a precious yellow metal from her breast, and pump the blood from her veins to power great machines.

A fifth man prayed for the elders, for he said that in the culture to come they would have little respect, that the stories of creation and of guidance would die out, and that people would lose their way.

A sixth man prayed for the women of his own tribe and the women of the culture to come, for they were the hope of the world, he said, and would be the first to follow the road back to beauty and harmony.

The pipe passed to me. With it I felt an infusion of deep grief, as visions of the holocaust of Native America flooded my mind. At the same time, I felt almost unbearable joy, as visions of a new world and a new culture incorporating the wisdom of these ancient people began to rise within my heart. I, too, prayed for the Native People and for my own culture— black, white, red, and yellow people mixed in the crucible of a new land, unified and made whole under the Great Tree of Peace by the wisdom of their red brothers and sisters. I prayed for strength and guidance to do what I could to bring about the new world. Then I handed the pipe to the elder, whose name sent a thrill up my spine. He was called Chasing Deer, the family name of my roommate, Tommy.

Chasing Deer took the pipe in his gnarled hands, and for an instant, he seemed to shift shapes into a tree whose roots were entwined in the bones of Grandmother Earth, and whose branches nearly touched the sun. I felt a bolt of energy surge through that ancient tree and connect the Earth and sky with a luminous rainbow.

Chasing Deer prayed for those in the Spirit World, and he prayed that all people, of all times, would have the ears to hear their guidance. He prayed for the Earth and all her creatures, the two-leggeds and four-leggeds, the winged ones, those who swim and those who creep. He prayed for the three sisters—the corn, beans, and squash—and for all that grows. He prayed for forgiveness between all who were oppressors and all who were oppressed. And then he prayed for me—that I have the courage to act upon my vision.

When our prayers were finished, Chasing Deer lit the pipe, and we passed it around the circle. Above our heads, I saw the prayers ascend on the smoke to the Above Beings who are always watching, ready to guide and help when we approach them with a humble heart and a desire to serve.

When the pipe was empty and the prayers had risen, I was overtaken by a deep sense of peace, and I dozed off. Sometime later, I awakened in the embrace of the Grandfather Tree, with the smell of the mossy forest in my nostrils and the music of the stream in my ears.

The shadows were getting long, and the afternoon was nearly spent before John felt ready to leave the stream and return to the house. Tommy was sitting in the sunroom, a spacious indoor garden filled with orchids, gardenias, and rare rain forest plants that John's mother had collected over many years, and which Jessie tended as lovingly as she did his mother's other children. The air smelled spicy, and was heavy with a humidity that was somehow rejuvenating, even in the June Virginia heat. Tommy said nothing as John entered the room, and they sat in silence for a long time. Finally, John spoke and told him of the dream. Oddly, Tommy didn't seem the least bit surprised.

"The Spirits have called you, Johnny-O. That's how it works. Tell me, was Chasing Deer wearing anything special around his neck?"

"He was, Tommy. I noticed it right away. It was the foot of a bird—the claws seemed almost luminescent."

Tommy nodded, and a smile lit up his eyes. "That's an owl

foot. That necklace has been in our family for hundreds of years. Tell me, when do you leave for Europe?"

John's eyes grew big as he realized that the dream existed not only in some other world, but had correspondences in this one. "Well, I'm due to leave about ten days after our vacation is done here."

"That doesn't leave us much time then, unless you can change your plans. We need to go to South Dakota soon. Chasing Deer will be waiting for us."

CHAPTER TWO

THE MEETING

Out in the wilderness, silence has its own sound. If you can quiet the chatter of your mind, you will hear the heartbeat of Mother Earth, the gentle voice of Windwoman as she caresses the leaves, and the conversation of the trees and animals. John and Tommy rode companionably in such a silence, their senses open to one another and to the strong bodies of their horses who moved in rhythm with their own young selves.

Leaving the world of airplanes and cities, radios and television, computers and term papers, they felt themselves drawn into an older, more primal cadence—a shift in time. The two friends rode from noon until late afternoon along a well-worn mountain trail, crossing small brooks where their horses drank, and refreshing themselves on the ride to the remote summer camp in the sacred Black Hills where Tommy's great-grandfather, the 118-year-old Chasing Deer, kept the archives of his people's prophecy.

The hot June sun filtered through the boughs of ancient spruce trees, and the clean fragrance of sage rose from the soft forest floor. As they entered a clearing, a carpet of red Indian paintbrush and delicate daisylike chamomile flowers seemed to shimmer with life. John's eyes filled with tears as he thought, *How is it that the world is so full of beauty, so full of life, and I have never really seen it before?*

His heart was at once filled with gratitude and also with grief for all he had missed. As Tommy looked over at him, John knew that his friend understood exactly what he was feeling, and his sense of kinship with the universe expanded into an uncanny sense of déjâ vu.

At just that moment, the pair arrived at a small log cabin, which seemed to glow in the rosy light of the late afternoon sun. Sitting outside on a sturdy bench made from a half log resting on two stumps, its surface worn smooth over time, was the oldest man that John had ever seen. He knew instantly that this was Chasing Deer, the keeper of the archives, and the old man he had met in his dream.

The owl's-foot necklace hung from Chasing Deer's neck, the black claws catching glimmers of light. *How could it be,* he wondered silently, *that we've never met, and yet it feels like I have always known and loved this man?* Once again, John's eyes filled with tears as he and Tommy got down from their horses and tied them to a rail on the west side of the cabin.

Chasing Deer walked briskly to them, and although he limped slightly as a result of being thrown from a horse nearly 25 years before, he exuded vitality. His craggy face was mobile, as if every emotion that John was experiencing registered there. Yet the strongest emotion that played across his features was a joyful kindness, a profound good humor born of having seen so much suffering, yet retaining hope and love rooted in a larger view of the universe. His long gray hair fell free over an old plaid shirt, neatly tucked into a pair of faded dungarees. He looked at John and Tommy, a smile crinkling up the corners of his deep obsidian eyes, and he began to chuckle.

"Hau, Grandfather." Tommy embraced him and then backed up to look him over. "You look terrible, ugly as ever."

Chasing Deer pulled himself up to his full six feet and placed his large hands on his hips. "And you, Grandson, look like your behind has been pounded raw by that old horse of Will's that you borrowed to get up here. You are getting too soft back East, up in that Ivory Tower where you study."

John's eyes grew wide as the insults flew back and forth, until both men turned to him, laughing. "Kidding each other like that is how we show affection, Johnny-O." Tommy stretched his lanky frame and brushed long black hair out of his eyes. "John," he said, with an extravagant gesture of his hand, "this is my great-grandfather, Chasing Deer."

He continued the introduction. "Grandfather," Tommy used the simple honorific term as he bowed toward John, "this is my esteemed former college roommate, John—dreamer of big dreams."

Chasing Deer took both of John's young hands into his old, lined ones and looked deeply into his eyes. "Welcome. I have been waiting for you. You were called here by the power of your dreaming, by your wish to serve, and so we have much to share. Please, just call me Grandfather, and I will call you Grandson. My speech may be formal, for English is not my first language, and I have learned much of it from books, but my heart is not so formal. That, I think, you already know."

Dropping John's hands, he smiled broadly, revealing an unlikely set of strong, perfect teeth. With a welcoming gesture to the two young men, he turned toward the cabin. "Come, my grandsons, you must be hungry from your long ride. I have cooked a pot of my specialty, buffalo stew, filled with many vegetables. Since my mate, Angela, passed into the Spirit World, it is about all I ever eat. Get your saddle bags, see to the horses, and we will settle down for supper and a sharing of stories."

John's face betrayed his thoughts. He was indeed starved, but the thought of eating buffalo was less than inviting. Chasing Deer laughed at him. "Grandson, stop worrying. You are in for a treat. Buffalo is delicious—like steak, but without the fat. It will not clog up those young arteries, and soon you will wish that they served buffalo burgers back East. Someday you will be 118 like me if you eat the buffalo and the other good gifts our Grandmother Earth provides, instead of all that pizza and soda that you young people think of as food."

Smiling now, John followed Chasing Deer and Tommy into the cabin, where they carried their small packs of clothing and other belongings. The air in the cabin was redolent of burned sage and the rich aroma of the stew. The fading light streamed through the small windows and illuminated the rich patina of the old wooden logs. The main room of the cabin was a combined kitchen and living area. The stew bubbled on a wood-fired stove, and biscuits were baking in the oven. There was a big porcelain sink, but no running water.

Chasing Deer handed an old tin bucket to John. "The well is around the east side of the house, Grandson. Please fetch us some water for coffee."

Tommy set the table, and when John returned, he put down the bucket of water and began to rifle through his pack, looking for the pouch of tobacco that he had brought as a gift of respect for Chasing Deer. The old man was measuring out coffee into a saucepan for the traditionally strong cowboy brew. When he had finished at the stove and settled down at the hand-hewn kitchen table, John walked over to the elder and shyly held out the tobacco.

"Grandfather, I'm honored that you invited me here. I'm also nervous because I don't know exactly what to say or do. Our worlds and our customs are different. I know that you have devoted your life to serving your people and creating an archive of their wisdom. I hope I can honor that wisdom and find ways to better serve my own people and all people. *Mitakuye Oyasin,*" he ended, clumsily repeating the Lakota term for "all my relations" that Tommy had taught him.

He proffered the pouch to the open hands of the old Indian. Chasing Deer looked at John solemnly and replied, "Hau," without taking the tobacco. John drew the pouch back toward his chest and again repeated, "*Mitakuye Oyasin,*" offering the tobacco to the elder. They repeated this exchange, according to custom, until Chasing Deer accepted the tobacco the fourth time it was offered.

"Your heart is good, Grandson. This I know, and it is why you are here. Please do not worry about offending me. Customs can be learned. But a good heart is the gift of Wakan Tanka, The Great Mysterious, or what some call The Great Spirit. You are my honored guest and family. My home is yours."

While the coffee boiled, Chasing Deer showed John around the cabin. Other than the kitchen/sitting room, furnished with a handsome wooden table, a threadbare once-green sofa, two old easy chairs, and a stained porcelain bathtub with clawfeet but no running water, there was a small bedroom with a chest of drawers and a mattress on the floor, and three much more spacious rooms.

All of these rooms were lined with shelves, extending from floor to ceiling, housing several thousand books, some hundreds of years old and others newly arrived from publishing houses. The topics ranged from American Indian studies to medicine and philosophy. One room boasted a wall of tall filing cabinets, filled with assorted papers and notes. Another room contained two large oak chests filled with photographs of ancient wampum belts and buffalo skins on which the stories of different tribes had been inscribed in pictographs. On the wall above the chests hung just such an enormous buffalo hide, stained with natural pigments that had held their color through countless returns of Grandfather Sun. John was anxious to hear the story that it told but knew enough not to ask. He would wait until Chasing Deer offered to tell him—if, indeed, that time ever came.

When the three men had finished their supper and washed the dishes, Chasing Deer took them to the talking place, a tipi where he smoked his pipe and prayed. It was here that he and John would meet for several hours a day over the next week.

The floor of the tipi was dirt, hardpacked and swept clean. A gutter system dug around the periphery of the structure sufficed to keep it dry inside. There was a firepit in the center of the floor, and the area around it was covered with several of what, to John, appeared to be fine old Navajo rugs.

Bundles of large-leafed sage, wild oregano, cedar, braids of sweet grass, and other herbs for cleansing and healing hung from the poles, and a bundle of Chasing Deer's sacred objects rested on a low stool, lovingly carved from a piece of lightning-struck aspen. The silence inside the tipi was even deeper than in the woods. It was as if the voices of the ancestors perpetually called from this sacred space, bidding those within to remember the wisdom that all life is holy, and that holiness is in relationship. *Mitakuye Oyasin*—all my relations.

It was in this timeless, sacred space that John recorded the conversations with Chasing Deer that are excerpted in this book. Like any college student, he came armed with notebooks, and with Chasing Deer's permission took careful notes on a wide range of subjects—the family, the environment, community, health, the holocaust of the American Indians, and some of the prophecies that foretold both the decimation of the original cultures of the Americas and their rebirth as part of a new integral culture—with the help of the very Euro-Americans who had once been the oppressors.

As you read these conversations, imagine that you, too, are sitting in the tipi with John and Chasing Deer and have purified the space with sage, cedar, and sweet grass. Imagine that you, too, have offered your prayers to the four directions, to Grandmother Earth, Grandfather Sky, and Wakan Tanka, and have smoked the *chanupa*—the sacred pipe. Imagine that the voices of the ancestors are speaking to you, bidding you to remember that we all are part of the circle, all related.

18

CHAPTER THREE

DREAMS AND PROPHECIES

John's first conversation with Chasing Deer took place in late June—at the time of the summer solstice when Grandfather Sun is at the highest point in the heavens and the days are the longest, when Grandmother Earth is creating new life and the winds are warm with the promise of a bountiful harvest. On the morning of the second day of his visit, Tommy left to return to the reservation and resume his apprenticeship with Fox Running, the medicine carrier who was his teacher.

So, with one another for company, Chasing Deer and John arose each morning to the harmony of birdsong and to the sun rising once again, renewing their bodies and the body of Grandmother Earth in whose womb we are nurtured all our lives. They greeted the sun with their prayers and smoked the sacred pipe in honor of the Directions. To the East they honored the blacktail deer people, to the South the owl people, to the West the buffalo people, and to the North the elk people. They honored Grandmother Earth, Grandfather Sky, and the Thunder Beings. And, of course, Wakan Tanka, The Great Mysterious.

Day by day, John began to feel knit back into the fabric of creation, at one with the spirits of the directions, the animals, and

Chasing Deer. Their friendship began to fill the inner emptiness that had become even more apparent as John sat beneath Grandfather Willow and dreamed of that time in the distant past, a time of peace and community when meaning came not from what one produced, but from relationships with other people, to The Great Mysterious, and to the Circle of Life. The dream had taught him that if one is oppressed, all are oppressed. If we pollute the Earth, we pollute ourselves. Even if most of us have forgotten the interdependence of life, if there are even a few who remember, that wisdom will rise again.

As John and Chasing Deer talked, sharing long periods of silence out of which words of deeper wisdom surfaced, they sat either in the tipi or on an old fallen log by a small stream whose music was a constant companion. Since Chasing Deer was a scholar as well as a storyteller, he often disappeared to fetch a book or a set of papers. It was during these absences that his words often found a deeper home within John's heart—or in the dreamtime, whose gossamer web blended past and future for the young man who came to find his vision and his destiny. This may happen for you as well, in the silent moments of the day and the night.

Chasing Deer may seem brusque at times because Indians are straightforward. They do not varnish the truth, but seek to speak in a clear manner. As you read his words, you cannot see the gentleness and strength that give his craggy face such character, or the twinkle in his old, clear eyes. But perhaps you can imagine how it may have been.

[**From the editor:** Please note that John's questions and observations are in italics throughout the rest of the text, followed by Chasing Deer's responses.]

John: Grandfather, I want to know more about the dream—or was it a vision?—that brought me here. It was so real, as real as sitting with you now. And yet you were there in the dreamtime, with your owl's-foot necklace. How can that be? Can a person be in two places at once? Was what I saw even a real place at some time in the past before that tribe was destroyed by the invasion of my ancestors?

Chasing Deer: Your dream was a gift from the Above Beings, an answer to your prayers, Grandson. Was it real in the sense that it had an existence that could be verified by others? It was real to me, for I dreamed that dream with you. But for me, the dream came three months before it came to you.

But I don't understand, Grandfather. You're blowing my mind. How could you have dreamed the same dream anyway, months before I did? And the village of Indians in my dream was on the East Coast at a time before the Europeans came. You come from the West and live in a different time.

Logic will not help you here, Grandson. The Spirit World works according to its own laws, and most of those are a Mystery. Suffice it to say that what we consider reality, that is, the logical consistency of temporal events, is missing in that world. In the Spirit World, one's intention—one's heart—is the prime mover, not time as we know it. In the Spirit World, we go where the heart leads us, and time becomes irrelevant, as does place. Do you remember when I shifted shapes in the dream, John, and became a tree? Am I really a tree?

I don't know what to think you are, Grandfather, but I know that you're a good man. When you shifted into a tree at the end of the dream, I felt like you were a bridge between heaven and Earth, past and future. Is that what you are?

I am if you make me so through your actions, Grandson. For which of us stands alone? All our intentions and actions are magnified or reduced, carried on or cut off by the actions of others. All creation is synergy and resonance. I am who I am in part because of who you are, and the Future that is calling you.

Future as in destiny? I don't know if I believe in destiny, Grandfather. I've thought some about it. If there's a destiny for every person, what's the point of living—I mean, if we can't change anything? We're just pawns of the Creator. What about free will?

Did anyone force you to pack up like a house on fire, leave Briarley in the flash of an eye, ride up to this place on horseback, and resign yourself to eating buffalo stew with an old Indian? You responded to the call of Spirit with your own free will. Had you not, a different future would have come into being, and you would have followed a different trail.

I've really been disturbed by the future that I saw in the dream, Grandfather. I saw the gentle people of that village being destroyed, and the Earth, too. And that future has indeed come to pass for your people. And from the little I know about American Indian prophecy, a similar future of destruction is in store for my own people.

Perhaps, Grandson. And perhaps not. You cannot change the past for my people, but you can help create a different future for all the children of the Earth. That is the value of prophecy. It warns only of a probable future, awakening the hearts of those who truly hear their deepest intention.

A man's intention is revealed by whom or what he chooses to serve. Will he serve himself, separate from others, or will he serve the Creator and the whole of life? When intention is strong, it is like unleashing a mighty wind that can reshape the landscape in a moment's time. Hitler, for example, had strong intention, but it was in the service of his own fears and need for power. Mother Teresa, too, had strong intention. But it was in the service of life.

I do want to serve life, Grandfather. It feels so strong, actually, this intention to serve. I can feel it in my body and in a connection to the Earth. I mean, I've always loved Briarley and the old Grandfather Willow Tree. But as I entered the dream, the tree felt alive to me, like we shared a consciousness. I remember wanting to pray the morning of the dream, and wondering how. Then I felt called to reach down and touch the Earth. That was my prayer, and I believe I heard her speak to me. We established a kind of relationship.

You have just defined prayer, Grandson. For it is a relationship with our Creator and all creation. Speaking to Grandmother Earth and to the trees, whom we call The Standing Praying Ones, is perfectly natural. My people commune with many aspects of Grandmother Earth—the trees and the elements, the animals and the stones, who are the oldest of Grandmother's children. What else did Grandfather Willow tell you?

When I found myself resting in the embrace of the tree after waking up from the dream, something kept telling me that Tommy held the key to its meaning. No, telling isn't strong enough. Something was urging me, pushing me to find him and reveal the whole thing, even though another part of me wanted to keep the dream inside for a while and tell no one.

Tommy and I have been close since the day we met, you know. And I don't mean close like it's ever been with anyone else. When I talk with Tommy, it's as if we feel each other's thoughts and emotions, like there's only one of us. The experience with the tree was like that.

The voice of The Great Mysterious is everywhere—in the winds, the water, the plants, the trees, the animals, the stones. In the voices of friends and strangers. In the patterns of the clouds. When you hear that voice, you might call it intuition. It is a call to alertness, to wake up and take action, which you did, so that harmony and balance can be restored. That is good, Grandson.

Do not take offense, but so many of your young people seem lost, and they seem to think that we old Indians have something to offer them. We do. But they are not the kinds of things that you can learn in a weekend workshop. Nor do we have dogma or creeds to teach or indoctrinate anyone with. What we do have is a deep spiritual life that is wholly embedded in the Earth and in our culture. It is not separate from our daily lived life. Few Euro-Americans can really understand us, or feel as we feel. Imagine talking to a tree in your world. You would be locked up in no time flat, I am sure of that.

Grandfather Willow has spoken to you, which means he believes that you have the ears to hear. And I believe as the willow. So feel comfortable here, Grandson. I will help you in any way I can, but you will have to do the work. To hear me you must see through the eye of the heart, for what goes through the mind only is not truly alive. Do you understand me?

I think so, Grandfather. Since I've been here, it seems like my senses are expanded. Like when I hear the sound of the brook or watch the little waterfall, I feel the water in my body. Like an emotion. Is that what you mean by seeing through the eye of the heart?

You speak truly, Grandson. When you see through the eye of the heart, wisdom is embodied—literally—in the body. The mind may tell you one story, but listening to the heart is another matter. Let us say that you meet a pretty girl, and your mind says that she might make a good mate. Yet you notice your stomach tensing up. Your body, your insides, are telling you something else. If you listen to your body, you will likely save yourself a lot of trouble. Wisdom is already within you about where a relationship with that girl might lead.

That is seeing through the eye of the heart, heeding the voice of Spirit. If you would prefer to think of it as intuition, that is the same thing. Dreams like the one you had beneath Grandfather Willow are a kind of embodied wisdom, a seeing through the heart. That dream is still alive in your body, Grandson, is that right? You think of the scenes and your body responds?

It sure does, Grandfather. I dreamed of a peace and a joy, as well as a deep sorrow, that are now part of me. Have your people ever had dreams or visions that have opened the eye of their heart? Are there stories, or even prophecies, that you can share with me?

Many, Grandson, for these dreams and prophecies are our lifeblood. Let me start with a prophecy from my mother's people. I think it wise that you know something of our past before we get to the present, for this is the information you will need to be most fully of service. As Tommy must have told you, my mother was Tsistsistas, or Cheyenne, as the Whites call us, and my father was Lakota, or Sioux, as we are known to others. Give me a minute to go and get some books and notes in case I need them. I will be right back.

Chasing Deer: Grandson, I am going to tell you the story of Sweet Medicine, the Cheyenne cultural hero, redeemer, and prophet. I will recount his life in some detail so that you may have a better feel for our people. I have brought much to read to you, quotes that you, as a student, should enjoy, for books—like stories—can be a great source of wisdom. According to the ancient Cheyenne elder, John Stands in Timber, Sweet Medicine was "the Sacred One who brought us our religion and told us what would happen to us. He is the Great One who came to our people long ago."

The cultural heroes of our people are not unlike those of Judaism and Christianity. Their relationship to the tribe is similar to that of Moses and the prophets in Judaism; and those of Jesus and the various New Testament prophets such as John, who wrote the Book of Revelation. But Sweet Medicine's prophecies differ from those of many Western prophets because they are clear as glass, leaving little room for interpretation or misunderstanding.

Before the coming of Sweet Medicine, the Cheyenne people had lapsed into a moral and spiritual decline. Self-centered and community-destroying behavior, including murder, had become the order of the day. Much of the behavior and social customs associated with American Indian tribalism was falling away. As John Stands in Timber recounts it, his people were truly savage at that time, unlike the gentle Cheyenne the White man was to encounter many centuries later.

One night, a young woman still living with her parents had an unusual dream. In it, she heard a Spirit Voice say, "Sweet Medicine shall come to you." The dream occurred on three successive nights and began to worry the young woman. After the fourth occurrence, she told her parents. They made light of the dream, telling her to think nothing of it. So there must have been something in the dream that disturbed them, Grandson, for our people do not take dreams lightly.

The dream spirit had spoken true in a way that neither the young woman nor her parents had expected, for the young woman was soon with child. Her parents were filled with embarrassment because their daughter was unwed, and they kept the pregnancy from the tribe.

When the young woman's time came, she went down to the

creek alone to have her child in seclusion. She built a small shelter and placed the healthy baby boy within it, hoping to avoid the shame of being found out. Not long after, an old woman went to the creek to gather grasses for the soft bedding they provided. She heard what she thought was a baby crying, but dismissed it thinking that it was just other people gathering grass. But the crying continued and no one was in sight, so the old woman followed the sound of the cries to their source. There she found the abandoned newborn and took him to her tipi to show her old husband. To her surprise, the old man raised his hands to the heavens proclaiming, "It is our grandson, and we shall name him Sweet Medicine."

The old couple found a nursing mother, and with her help, raised the baby. He grew quickly into a strong young lad outstripping the other boys of his age in the tribe. And at the tender age of ten, Sweet Medicine performed his first miracle.

Times were lean for the Cheyenne, food was scarce, and the buffalo were hard to find. So Sweet Medicine went to his grandmother and asked her for a buffalo hide that he had her prepare according to his instructions. When that was done, he asked her to make a hoop from a cherrywood bough. Next, he asked her to make four pointed cherrywood sticks with forks of one, two, three, and four prongs. When the buffalo skin was properly prepared and cut into one long strip, it was used to make, along with the hoop, a net with a center hole, not unlike a dream catcher.

By this time, the People were wondering what Sweet Medicine and his grandmother were up to. He went to the center of the village with his grandmother, taking all the objects that she had made according to his instructions. The tribe gathered around him in a circle. While his grandmother brought the hoop to the center of the circle, Sweet Medicine laid out his sharpened sticks in a row. When he picked up the first stick, the one with the single fork, his grandmother rolled the hoop, crying, "My Grandson, here is a yellow buffalo calf," and Sweet Medicine threw the first stick at the rolling hoop. The hoop fell over. Sweet Medicine and his grandmother repeated this with the next two sticks until only the fourth stick was left. When the hoop was rolled the fourth time, Sweet Medicine sent his last stick cleanly through the center hole, and the hoop changed into a young buffalo with an arrow in its side. The People were told to get the meat they needed, which they did until all had had their fill.

What an incredible story, Grandfather. It reminds me of Jesus feeding the multitudes with a few fish and a basket of bread. Or even God providing manna from heaven when Moses was leading the Jews out of Israel and they were wandering in the desert for those 40 years before they reached the Promised Land.

That is why I told you that the tale of Sweet Medicine and his role had some similarities to Judeo-Christian stories. The full story of Sweet Medicine would take many hours to recount, so I am going to skip much of it and pick up again when he was still a young man and needed a new buffalo robe, bringing about an unfortunate incident that led to a long exile from the tribe. Just as Jesus had to be alone for 40 days in the wilderness, and the Jews had to wander for 40 years, Sweet Medicine, too, had to endure a lengthy time apart from his people, learning to overcome anger and listen to the Voice of The Great Mysterious so that he could bring healing to his people.

One day there was a successful hunt with many buffalo killed, so Sweet Medicine decided to return to the same grassy plains to find just the right buffalo for his new robe. He spied the animal he wanted and deftly sent an arrow deep into its side. As he began to skin the buffalo and prepare the meat, an old man approached him—some say he was a chief—saying that the hide of this particular buffalo was exactly what he had been looking for. He insisted that Sweet Medicine give it to him. Sweet Medicine refused to give up the hide, but offered the old man all the succulent meat. But the old man continued to insist on having the hide, claiming that if it was not given to him, he would take it. At last Sweet Medicine was overcome by anger and struck the old man with a severed buffalo foot, knocking him unconscious.

Now there are few transgressions graver than an act of violence against an elder. Soon the warriors of the tribe set out in search of Sweet Medicine. But while they could find his tracks, they could not find Sweet Medicine, for he was a shape-shifter and could assume the body of an animal. This made him impossible to catch. Finally, after many years, the chiefs asked Sweet Medicine's brother to go find him and tell him that he could return to the People. His brother did so, and the two went on a successful buffalo hunt. But when the brother returned to camp for dogs to carry back the meat, there were still many who did not want Sweet Medicine back, so the brother abandoned him and the buffalo on the plains.

Two years later, the People relented, and the brother once again found Sweet Medicine, who was so angry that he would neither talk to his brother nor even look at him. In desperation, his brother sent Sweet Medicine's elderly parents to ask him to come home. But it was no use. Sweet Medicine remained silent, and no pleas could reach his heart.

Four years later, Sweet Medicine came across some young boys gathering rushes and grasses for their people to eat. The buffalo had grown scarce and the People were very hungry. Sweet Medicine asked the boys to go and get him some bark from the inside of an elm tree. When they returned, Sweet Medicine took the bark and turned it into meat for the boys to eat. After they had eaten, Sweet Medicine directed them to take the rest of the meat back to the camp and to tell the People that it was from him.

The tribe had grown weary and hungry during the years that Sweet Medicine was gone. The chief was so grateful to have food for his hungry people that he sent two runners to ask Sweet Medicine to return, but this time with an offer of the hand of the chief's daughter. Sweet Medicine returned, wed the beautiful young woman, and lived for many happy years with the People as they prospered, due to his wise counsel and constant care.

Quite some time later, Sweet Medicine and his wife announced that they were going on a journey and might be gone for a while. It was during this journey to the Black Hills that Sweet Medicine received his instructions from the Spirit World and was given the four sacred arrows of the People. From that time forward, Sweet Medicine instructed the People about what he had been taught and brought a new ceremonial life to them.

Now I can answer some of your questions about prophecy, Grandson. So listen carefully. After a long life of over 100 years, Sweet Medicine called the tribe to him, for he was greatly troubled and knew that his time on Earth was drawing to a close.

Sweet Medicine told the gathered tribe that he had given them the instructions that they should live by and that only if they continued to follow those instructions would they remain strong. But should they fall from those ways, all manner of trouble would beset them. This said, Sweet Medicine delivered this prophecy:

> There are many people on this Earth besides the Cheyenne and their Indian brothers. At some time, many people that you know nothing of shall come from the East. Some of them shall be black, but there will be a fair-skinned people, and they shall be numerous. These fair-skinned ones shall have hair much lighter than yours, and they shall have hair upon their face. Their customs and manners shall be very different from yours. They will come with their own ways of thinking, and they shall not pray to the Great-Grandfathers as you do. Listen to nothing that they say. But, I fear that, trusting them, you will listen.
>
> These fair-skinned ones are a restless people, and they are never satisfied. They do not know what it is to be content and grateful for all that the Great-Grandfathers and Grandmother Earth have provided. They will move quick-

ly from one place to another, ever pushing forward, and more and more of them shall come. They shall not come to you only on foot, but also in strange things upon the rivers and in boxes across the land. Their clothing shall not be like yours, but rather made of many pieces together and in many pretty colors.

They shall offer you many things, like isinglass (a reflective object, the White man's mirror). All that they offer you will do you no good and will begin to sap both the strength and the will of the People. Their food shall be strange, and they shall offer you something like sand to eat that shall be very sweet. Eat nothing that they give you, for none of it will be good for you. But worst of all, they will offer you a strange drink, and if you drink it, you will go crazy. Unfortunately, you will like these things that the Earth Men bring, and more than likely you will take them. I warn you that, if you do, your troubles will be never-ending. Take nothing from them. But I fear for you, and my heart is very heavy.

These people will kill the animals and will uproot the Earth. The buffalo will be hunted down for sport. Our four-legged brothers and sisters will begin to disappear. They shall hunt them with a strange and powerful weapon; the new weapon shall be noisy and from it will be sent something like a pebble, which will be deadly. When they come, they will bring with them their own kind of animal—not like the buffalo, but with short, shiny hair, white horns, and split hooves. These animals they will eat and so will you. There is another kind of animal that they shall bring, one with a long tail and hair about its neck. This animal will allow you to travel far. With the coming of this animal, your decline shall begin. That is what I fear.

These people do not love the Grandmother Earth as you do. They will dig her up and fly in Her air. They may even take thunder from the sky so that where they live they can see at night. Ceaselessly they will search for a certain stone that our Great-Grandfather has placed upon the Earth. They do not follow the ways of the Great-Grandfather, and they will dig and dig into the Earth to find this stone. They will kill our Grandmother Earth.

I see unknown sicknesses coming to you. You will die off. Maybe all of you will die. And worst of all, if any of you do survive, these people will want your flesh, the very children of the People. This you must never let happen. For, if you do, your children will become like them, and they will know nothing. These people are relentless and will do all in their power to make you like them. They will not stop.

My heart is saddened, for you will not remember what I have said to you—you will leave your religion for something new. You will lose respect for your leaders and start quarreling with one another. You will lose track of your relations and marry women from your own family. You will take after Earth Men's ways and forget the good things by which you have lived, and in the end become worse than crazy.

I am sorry to say these things, but I have seen them, and you will find that they come true.

Fearing that all this should come to pass, Sweet Medicine gave his last instruction to the People: "The last women among you must carry the sacred arrows to a high hill and lay them down for a time when the People shall return to the Earth."

That, Grandson, is a brief account of the life of Sweet Medicine and his dying prophecy. What do you think?

I think I need to read that again—it was so full of detail; it was amazing. Can I get copies of what you read me for my notes?

Of course, Grandson. Part of your work will be to tell the old stories so that you can inspire people to create new stories of renewal and care. I fear that I may sound gruff to you, but the

White man, what Sweet Medicine called the Earth Men, has destroyed both our People and the land with greed and short-sightedness, and in the end will destroy himself as well unless the hearts of your people undergo a spiritual awakening.

Don't worry, Grandfather. I know that you don't mean to be hurtful, only truthful. Sweet Medicine foresaw the destruction that my people brought in incredible clarity, but honestly, I was inspired by his ordinariness as much as by his prophetic powers. He had a lot of anger, and he made very human mistakes. But his life was a redemption of those mistakes, and the instructions he got for his People—I see that People is capitalized in the story— were also for him. And like you said, I've never heard a prophe-cy that was as lucid as Sweet Medicine's. Most of the ones in the Bible are pretty cryptic, and people have been arguing about their meanings for centuries. Sweet Medicine's prophecies have all basically come true.

But tell me something, Grandfather. This still bothers me. The things we were talking about before—the difference between destiny and free will. I've always thought that prophecies aren't absolute, I mean, like written in stone. So that while they may tell what will happen if a certain course is followed, couldn't they also help us choose a different path?

That is so, Grandson. But the problem, as I see it, is this: Prophecies are generally about major directions in a people's his-tory. They are not about trivial things, but matters that may affect the entire course of a culture's future. Now here is the trouble. By the time a critical situation is reached, people are so embedded in the kinds of thinking, values, and behavior that led to the critical point that nothing less than a heroic effort on the part of the pop-ulation as a whole can sway the course of events. This is particu-larly true of a culture like yours that places great value on such things as power and wealth, or anything, for that matter, except the spiritual and the moral. It is easy for a people to become blind to what is right and live in fear of losing material goods.

I think that you're right, Grandfather, but aren't there other things that can change a nation's course? Sometimes the agents of destruction or change may come from outside. For instance, if the Holocaust had been prophesied for the Jews, what could they have done to stop it? The Nazis and their armies were far too strong for the Jews to have done much.

You can kill try to kill a people, Grandson, but if the light of their spiritual life continues to burn inside of them, then they shall continue. This has been the way of the Jews all through history, through many attempted destructions, and I admire them greatly for it. You would have to kill every last one to eliminate Judaism, and even then, other people might adopt and continue the teachings. This is exactly what is happening with American Indian culture. People of other colors and traditions are adopting our ways.

Were there any other prophecies about the destruction or the resurrection of your culture?

Today and tomorrow we will talk of the destruction, Grandson. On the next day we will hear the vision of His Crazy Horse, who speaks of a resurrection of all Nations of the Earth, united under the Great Tree of Peace.

I will read you a prophecy from my father's people, the Lakota. This is one known well to all of us. I first heard it from my great-grandfather when I was a small boy. His name was Stands Alone, and he was born around 1785 and died in 1890 shortly after Wounded Knee. I think that massacre broke his heart. Black Elk, the Lakota holy man, told the prophecy of Drinks Water or Wooden Cup to the writer John G. Neihardt in the following way:

You people in the future remember all this land will be different. Likewise, you people will be different from what you are today. The day will come where I stand, you will stand. Then the people will never be in the hoop again. Remember this, too: They shall entangle the universe (world) with iron and when you get to that time you shall live in different tipis. Then you will come upon great differences. From where you are always facing and where the day breaks, different men are coming. They will fill this world. Those are the ones that will make this a different world. When you get there, there will be great wars. But, people, there is one thing. Remember your peace pipe; don't forget that, even when you come to the time I am telling about. Remember that. Maybe the Great-Grandfather (Mysterious One) might send his voice to you. And maybe our Grandmother the Earth might help us.

Drinks Water also predicted that the People would live in little gray square houses. I will tell you that there are many of those on the reservations and in Indian public housing in Rapid City. I cannot see those houses without thinking of Drinks Water. He also said that we would starve in these houses, Grandson, and indeed, many of our People are hungry. The destruction of the buffalo and other animals Drinks Water spoke of was the beginning of our hunger. The iron that he said would entangle the Earth must be the railroad tracks that spread like a cancer, bringing blight and ruin in their wake. John, have you ever been to a reservation and seen the poverty and desperate state of our people?

No, I haven't, Grandfather. But I've read about it, and I feel your people's pain. I truly do. That pain has been part of me ever since the dream. I'd like to help make a difference, to help end the suffering, but I don't know how yet. Perhaps it will be in my law practice. In my dream, I saw how the Indians from the part of Virginia that I come from must have lived once. I've never seen such contentment, joy, and laughter as I saw on the faces of those people.

I will tell you about some prophecies from the Eastern tribes who first encountered the White man, Grandson. Eastern tribes such as you saw in your dream.

According to the Wampanoag, who lived on the coast of what you now call Massachusetts, a deathbed vision came to an old and wise chief in which he saw a white whale. The old man told the people that the coming of the white whale was an omen of the coming of a white people. These white people would take the Indians' land and push them out. Even John Winthrop, a descendant of the early Massachusetts Bay Colony governor, reported in 1702 that there was a white whale living in a pond on the Elizabeth Islands where the Wampanoag once ranged.

A Powhatan medicine man from what is now called Virginia foretold that "bearded men should come & take their country & that there should none of the original Indians be left, within a hundred and fifty years." Around 1540, a group of Indians went to visit the Spanish explorer DeSoto's camp in Mississippi. I have never been able to find out if they were Choctaws, Tunicas, or Chickasaws. Nevertheless, according to the Spanish invaders, "they were come to see what people [the Spanish] were and that they had learned from their ancestors that a white race would inevitably subdue them."

The fact that tribes from different parts of the country all foresaw the coming of the White invaders, whether Spanish or other Europeans, is absolutely remarkable.

No matter how many times I tell these prophecies, Grandson, I, too, am always amazed. In the Midwest, an Ojibwa prophet had the following dream:

> Men of strange appearance have come across the great water. They have landed on our island [North America]. Their

skins are white like snow, and on their faces long hair grows. These people have come across the great water in wonderfully large canoes which have great white wings like those of a giant bird. The men have long and sharp knives, and they have long black tubes which they point at birds and animals. The tubes make a smoke that rises into the air just like the smoke from our pipes. From them come fire and such terrific noise that I was frightened, even in my dream.

In the Southwest, the Spanish explorer Coronado wrote down what a group of Zuni elders told him in 1540: "It was foretold more than fifty years ago that a people such as we are would come, and from the direction we have come, and that the whole country would be conquered."

Let me read to you from *The Book of Books of Chilam Balam*. The Maya of Mexico and Central America recorded this prophecy of their destruction at the hands of the Spanish:

> Scattered through the world shall be the women who sing, and the men who sing and all who sing. . . . No one will escape, no one will be saved. . . . There will be much missing in the years of the rule of greed. Men will turn into slaves. Sad will be the face of the sun. . . . The world will be depopulated, it will become small and humiliated.

So you see, Grandson, the prophecies of the coming of the White man and the destruction of our people and their cultures came from all over the Americas. There are many, many more, but they all say essentially the same thing. Things like airplanes, electricity, and the coming of missionaries were not foretold by Sweet Medicine alone. Some of these things, if not all, were seen in the prophecies of the Crow prophet Medicine-Raven, a Wet'suwet'en medicine man in midwestern Canada, and by the Southwestern Hopi in their prophecies.

How awesome and how terrible. I mean one prophecy could be dismissed maybe, but not such a large number of them.

Prophecies are not so astounding to our people, for they are not a thing of the distant past. They continue right through present times. I have lived with many medicine people and know their power. But it is getting late into the day, Grandson, and I would like to leave you with one last thought, reminding us that all things are interconnected. Many of the prophecies of future times yet to come predict a purification, a time of cleansing and upheaval for the Earth unless there is a radical change in our world. This only makes sense. The destroyers eventually become the destroyed, and so does the circle of life progress, because we are all joined in the Sacred Hoop.

Rest well tonight, Grandson, for tomorrow we will talk about what happened when the White man came to our shores.

CHAPTER FOUR

THE AMERICAN INDIAN HOLOCAUST

"I live in fear! There is no man I hate,
no matter who he is or what he is.
But I live in fear of the white man,
I fear the death he possesses. I fear
the violence that is in him. And I
would not be surprised if one day the
white man killed himself, and all of us.
I live in terrible fear of that."

— Vine Deloria, Sr., Yankton Sioux, 1968

Carl Jung spoke of synchronicities, little signs that the Universe is orderly and intelligent, when the outer world becomes a stunning mirror of our inner thoughts and feelings. You are thinking of someone, and a letter from that person arrives in the mail. You are researching old gardens, and a company you never heard of sends you a catalog with just the specimens you are looking for. John's time with Chasing Deer was punctuated by frequent synchronicities that made him feel as if The Great Mysterious was always present, and that there was a pattern and a purpose to his time with the grand old Indian elder.

The early days of their visit were sun-drenched and warm. A kind of joy emanated from the Earth and from her creatures—the birds and deer, the red fox whose black-stockinged feet and ears were a daily delight, the ants who industriously scurried to gather the bounty of the wildflowers. But on the day they were to speak of the American Indian holocaust, all of nature seemed to reflect the quiet melancholy that both John and Chasing Deer felt. The sky was sullen and heavy with unshed rain. The fox stayed in her den, as did the ants in their massive pine needle–topped mounds. The birds were still, and all of nature was preternaturally silent.

As the day wore on, the sun masked by dark and angry clouds, Chasing Deer read accounts of the beautiful cultures that had been cruelly wiped out by the Spaniards and other European nations. John felt a fire well up inside of him, deep in his belly. Indignation grew into a living thing, not only on account of the horrors that were inflicted on the indigenous tribes of the Americas, but on account of the holocausts that continue even now, all over the world.

Anger is energy. If it is turned inward, so they say, we feel depressed. If it is turned outward, we are prone to violence. Only in its transformation to compassion and ethical action is the energy redeemed and put to a higher use. In John's case, the Thunder Beings born in his belly that afternoon ignited the intention to direct his study of law so that he could defend American Indian rights and try to hold the government to the treaties that have been so shamelessly disregarded even to this day.

As his intention gathered form and power, jagged bolts of lightning sought the deposits of iron ore deep within Grandmother Earth. The landscape lit up, and the Thunder Beings spoke with a great voice, rumbling through the sky. The clouds opened and shed their tears on a willing Earth, who received them so that she could bear fruit. The longing that had brought John his dream, and his visit with Chasing Deer, was sanctified and sealed by his willingness to accept what he had begun to think of as his destiny.

John: It was hard to sleep last night, Grandfather. I kept waking up, catching the tails of my dreams. The young man who had spoken of the destruction of his people in the Big Dream, as I think of it, underneath Grandfather Willow, kept telling me more things about the destruction of his people, about the deaths of his wife and young son in a raid on their village. I can still feel his heartbreak.

Chasing Deer: You are a person deeply centered in your body, Grandon. For you, this is a clear road to inner wisdom. It is also a kind of telegraph line through which the Above Beings speak to you. But while it is among your greatest gifts, be careful that you do not store the anguish of others in your own bones, or you will lose your life-force energy and become sick. Say a prayer for that young man and his family, and then breathe out the sorrow so that your energy will be available here and now for what must be done, and for the joy and gratitude that are the foundation of life and health. Do you think you can practice that? Because if you cannot, we will have trouble getting through this long day of sad recollections together.

I know you're right, Grandfather. And if I understand you correctly, when I feel the emotions of others, I need to let them flow through me instead of hanging on to them. Otherwise I'll clog up my circuits and won't be of much use to anyone.

You understand me rightly, Grandson. I am not asking you to harden your heart, but to let it be as spacious as Grandfather Sky, and as generous of spirit. Compassion is the root of ethical action, but grief and sadness are like a heavy stone that blocks the good road to healing. Now, are you ready to begin?

I'm ready, Grandfather.

What do you know of holocausts?

Well, naturally I think of Nazi Germany and the brutal extermination of some six million Jews and a million or so Gypsies.

And tell me, were these Jews and Gypsies grandmothers and grandfathers, mothers and fathers, sons and daughters?

Yes, of course they were. The Nazis didn't care who you were as a person. If you were a Jew or some other seeming undesirable, you were to be wiped out, unless you could serve some purpose like slave labor. But then you were probably doomed to death anyway through overwork, lack of food, grief, medical experiments, and God knows what other kinds of abuse. The Nazis were fiends, and there was no end to the tortures they devised for human suffering.

So, simply because of one's religion and culture, one was doomed to a hideous death or, if lucky, enslavement?

It wasn't just that, Grandfather. For the Nazis it was a racial thing, too. They thought of the Jews and Gypsies as inferior races that would pollute the pure Aryan blood of their so-called master race.

Then it would be fair to say that for the Nazis, some races, some cultures, some people, were more entitled to live than others? And those unfortunate others were to be either exterminated or enslaved and dominated for the uses and purposes of the one true race and culture? Is that so?

That's certainly what the Nazis believed.

Let me ask you a question. If you were talking to a group of your people—no, let us say to a large group of fellow students when you were in college this past year, and you mentioned the word *Holocaust,* would they know what you were talking about?

Of course they would. Every educated person knows what Holocaust *refers to.*

This disturbs me greatly.

Disturbs you? Why would that disturb you, Grandfather? The Holocaust was the greatest display of inhumanity that there ever was, and that it occurred in relatively recent times is all the more terrifying. There's never been another thing like it in human history, and we need to remember it so that it never happens again. Just like we need to remember Hiroshima and Nagasaki. The images in my mind from the movies, pictures, and books I've read about the Holocaust are sickening, and that's as it should be. What would be disturbing is if we didn't remember it, if we pretended that it never happened, if we didn't try to understand the causes behind it.

How can we live in the truth of today and have hope for tomorrow if we don't know the past: where we have come from, what human beings are capable of, what must be protected against, and what must be avoided at all costs. A culture, a country, is like a person. There's no growth unless mistakes are recognized and some attempt is made to right previous wrongs. So, tell me, Grandfather, what could possibly be so disturbing to you about people remembering the Holocaust?

What is disturbing, Grandson, is this. And let me state before I begin that nothing of what I have to say is meant to minimize the horrors inflicted on the oppressed people under the Nazi Regime in Germany. It was hideous and truly beyond imagination for anyone with a shred of humanity in them.

What distresses me is that Americans are plagued by selective memory. The Holocaust inflicted by Nazi Germany on Jews and others is capitalized, as if it were the only one. What about the millions of Ukrainians starved to death by Stalin, the bloody invasion of Tibet by the Chinese, or the torture and killing of fellow Cambodians by Pol Pot? And closer to home, Grandson, although you and your classmates have studied years of American history in school, I doubt that many have any knowledge of the brutal destruction of the peoples native to the Americas by the colonial powers of Europe and by the United States, whose policy has always been to exterminate the Indians like vermin and take their lands.

While five to six million Jews perished during the Nazi Regime, it is estimated that 100 million Indians from the Caribbean, Central, South, and North America perished at the hands of the European invaders. Sadly, unbelievably, really, much of that wholesale destruction was sanctioned and carried out by the Roman Catholic Church and various Protestant denominations.

I'm sorry, Grandson, for I see that the color has left your cheeks, and I fear that the passion and empathy I feel for these murdered people has entered your body like an attack. This I do not mean, for you are not responsible for the deeds of your ancestors.

I do feel sick at heart, Grandfather. For in my case, it was truly my direct ancestors who were part of this Holocaust. And I do feel responsible. Not for their deeds, but for the cover-up and whitewash of history that prevents new generations from learning from the mistakes of the old. I have felt this sickness and responsibility growing, ever since the Big Dream, and I dread hearing the details that I know you're going to tell me today.

You are not responsible for what you did not know, Grandson. But starting today, you will have the responsibility to tell the truth so that some of the past wounds can be healed, and so that the past will not continue to repeat in the future. I know this is hard for you, but I want you to know the complete story. Do you still feel up to it? For now we will cover some truly shocking material.

Please continue, Grandfather. As you told me, I will try to keep breathing and let the horror wash through my heart, rather than letting it—what did you say?—get stuck in my bones.

All right, then. Perhaps you think that the close parallel between the genocide of Nazi Germany and what occurred in the Americas is an unlikely stretch. But, believe me, it is not. One only needs to read *Mein Kampf* in which Adolf Hitler wrote that the agenda for the ultimate triumph of Nazism was to follow the blueprint of the Catholic Church with its "traditional adherence to dogma" and its consequent "fanatical intolerance." Furthermore, Grandson, Hitler expressed his admiration for the "efficiency" with which the genocide of the Indian was carried out in the Americas. It was, in his view, "a forerunner" for his own "plans and programs."

Do you know the work of Elie Wiesel, a survivor of the Nazi Holocaust who has done so much to alert the world to the dangers of fanaticism and intolerance? What he wrote about the Nazis could just as easily have been written about any of the European invaders. Namely that: "All the killers were Christian. . . . The Nazi system was the consequence of a movement of ideas and followed a strict logic; it did not arise in a void but had its roots deep in a tradition that prophesied it, prepared for it, and brought it to maturity. That tradition was inseparable from the past of Christian, civilized Europe."

Let me read you what Stannard, a first-class historian, concludes: "Elie Wiesel is right: the road to Auschwitz *was* being paved in the earliest days of Christendom. But another conclusion is equally evident: on the way to Auschwitz the road's pathway led straight through the heart of the Indies and of North and South America."

Grandson, you are special, or I would not have you here. If I utter things that are harsh or hurtful to your ears, do not take them personally. When I refer to the White invaders, I am not indicting your race. Whether a person is Red, Black, Yellow, or White makes no difference. So when I talk about White culture, I am only referring to some of the blind spots of Western thought that can prevent a person's innate good-heartedness from shining through. And as you say, Grandson, we cannot change the future, or understand the prophecies that I will tell you tomorrow, until we have fully faced the past.

Grandfather, I'm almost totally in the dark about the conquest and the settlement of the Americas, in spite of years of education. But you've already said something that has me reeling in shock. How could Christianity, based as it is on love and compassion, possibly sanction genocide?

That is a crazy thing, isn't it, Grandson? But it is so easy to become blinded by dogma that religious teachings can function in complete opposition to the original instructions of the founders. You know that Holy Wars have blighted the Earth since the time of Christ. And those wars did not end in the Middle Ages.

Let me tell you about the coming of Columbus, celebrated as a hero by your people and reviled as a demon by mine. Perhaps you may remember that just as Columbus was sailing to the New World, the same King Ferdinand and Queen Isabella who commissioned his voyage issued an edict expelling all the Jews from Spain, upon pain of death, unless they converted to Catholicism. The Crown's consuming need for power was sanctified as the will of God. And this perversion of religion drove both the Jews from the Old World and the Indians from the New World.

There is a lot of material I wish to show you, Grandson. So please bear with a long-winded old man. First, let us look at the evidence about the life and moral character of the indigenous Americans. So often we are portrayed as savages in need of salvation or even as devils *beyond* salvation, and therefore subject to destruction as inhuman and inferior. Yet there is no account that I know of where the White man was not greeted with the greatest kindness and hospitality upon first encountering the indigenous peoples. I have volumes of firsthand accounts, Grandson, which you may want to copy later. For now, let us cover just a few. Columbus wrote about the native peoples to the Spanish sovereigns who sponsored his voyages:

> They are so artless and free with all they possess, that no one would believe it without seeing it. Of anything they have, if you ask them for it, they never say no; rather they invite the person to share it, and show as much love as if they were giving their hearts; and whether the thing be of value or of small price, at once they are content with whatever little thing of whatever kind be given to them.

Columbus thought that these people were a living expression of God, and the word *Indian* actually comes from the Spanish *in Deos,* or in God. What an oddity it was, then, that they were wiped out in the name of Christianity. Michele de Cuneo, a compatriot of Columbus on the Admiral's second voyage, wrote in a letter that when the ship anchored, the native people came out "to greet the ships with gifts of fish and fruit, as if we had been brothers."

In Columbus's logs from his first voyage, he is continually astounded by the kind and thoughtful ways of the people he meets. Here are a few excerpts: "And the people are all so gentle" (October 13, 1492).

And a week later we find, ". . . these are the friendliest people." Apparently this was true wherever he went, for two months later on December 21, 1492, he entered the following: "There cannot be better or more gentle people than these anywhere in the world. . . . The chiefs are men of few words and fine manners, it is a marvel."

In other entries, he comments on the cleanliness and comeliness of the people, of the beauty of their villages and their housing. In October 1492 he writes, "The houses of these Indians are the most beautiful I have ever seen. . . . They are well swept and quite clean inside, and the furnishings are arranged in good order."

So, even by the best of European standards, the natives were clean, mannerly, hospitable, and generous to a fault, an expression you would never find among our people, for generosity is a principal virtue. Interesting, don't you think, Grandson, how language reveals the values of a culture? I mean, what kind of a world is it where generosity can be seen as a fault at some point along a continuum? I have often wondered what Jesus or St. Francis would think about that.

Now, the experience of being greeted with kindness and generosity was substantially the same for all the Europeans arriving on these shores, whether it be in the Caribbean or on the continents. In 1584, the Englishman Arthur Barlowe, after arriving in what is now called Virginia and taking possession of the land for the Queen—of course, the Powhatans and other tribes living there were not consulted on the matter—wrote about his first encounter with the Indians:

> We were entertained with all love and kindness and with as much bounty, after their manner, as they could possibly devise. We found the people most gentle, loving and faithful, void of all guile and treason, and such as lived after the manner of the Golden Age . . . a more kind and loving people there can not be found in the world, as far as we have hitherto had trial.

Amerigo Vespucci, whom I am sure you read about in your history books, wrote that the natives were "a race I say gentle and amenable." He also wrote that "they live together without king, without government, each is his own master." But this kind of peaceful self-governing community was all too soon wiped out.

It sounds like the Americas were a kind of Garden of Eden. And truly, Grandfather, if you hadn't read all those notes to me, I would think that you were simply idealizing the past. Kind of glorifying the "noble savages," if you'll pardon the expression. Isn't it human nature to remember the better parts of life as time goes on, and to enshrine the good old days?

Believe me, Grandson, I have volumes more that you can read. When my wife was alive, I kept her up many a night reading this material. She finally—what is your expression—oh, yes, she said *uncle,* and then I had to keep my research to myself. So if I tend to share a lot of detail, you will understand that I have waited for receptive ears for many sun returns. In any case, Grandson, a few decades after Columbus arrived, the indigenous cultures he found had all but vanished.

It seems impossible, Grandfather. Are you sure? I recall that Columbus only had about 90 men on his voyage, and some of them were boys.

You are right. The real destruction began after his second voyage, which left for the Americas in 1493. This time there were 17 ships and about 1,200 men. The arriving Spaniards were shown the same kindness and humanity as on the previous voyage, but this decency was not reciprocated, and in a generation's time, millions of native peoples were dead, and nearly every Caribbean island thoroughly devoid of its original inhabitants.

My God—millions! I had no idea that there had been any-where near that many people in the Caribbean. I thought there were just a few small tribes scattered here and there, that the Americas were hardly inhabited at all. Tell me how all this came about, Grandfather. It wasn't in any of the history books that I've studied.

I will outline what happened. When Columbus returned from the Caribbean, the news of gold and a paradise spread like wild-fire across Europe. The Spanish Crown was under severe finan-cial stress, and the thought of untold fields of gold and wealth from commerce fired the Crown's imagination, not to mention the people's. Columbus was swamped with volunteers for the second voyage, unlike the first. And in short order, the imagina-tion of Rome was also fired, and the thought of converts and more wealth for the Church brought His Holiness, the Pope, and with him, of course, God onto the scene.

On May 3, 1493, Pope Alexander VI issued the infamous *Bull Inter Caetera,* which granted the monarchs of Spain the right to possess, own, and exploit any part of the Earth not already under the control of a Christian nation. Being "infallible," the Pope could do this with "certain knowledge and out of the fullness of our apos-tolic power, by the authority of Almighty God." The unsuspecting inhabitants of these unknown lands were to be brought into the Catholic fold and "trained in good morals." Naturally, this kind of thinking and greed soon spread throughout all of Europe.

For instance, King Henry VII, himself a devout Catholic, was not to be left out, so he granted a commission to John Cabot "to conquer, occupy and possess the lands of the 'heathens and infi-dels.'" Henry's expressed motive was simply to acquire "domin-ion, title and jurisdiction of the same." Here is where the geno-cide of the native peoples began in earnest, and over 500 years later it is still going on.

Armed with the blessings of the Church, Columbus traveled

to many Caribbean islands. In each place, he would read a fearsome document giving the Church and the Monarchy of Spain the right to seize the lands, and if necessary, kill the occupants. See here, Grandson. This is a document called the *Requerimiento*. As you can read, it states that the people must accept the truth of Christianity and unquestionably acknowledge the authority of both the Pope and the Monarchy of Spain.

That the people did not understand the Spanish tongue did not matter a whit to either Columbus or the subsequent conquistadors. Their "ignorance" of the language was apparently viewed as more evidence of their inferior nature. Acknowledgment and acceptance of the statements read to them was expected to be both complete and without hesitation or reservation. Were it not, which one can scarcely imagine it could be, since no one understood the meaning of the words, the following was then read:

> I certify to you that, with the help of God, we shall powerfully enter into your country and shall make war against you in all ways and manners that we can, and shall subject you to the yoke and obedience of the Church and Their Highnesses.
>
> We shall take you and your wives and your children, and shall make slaves of them, and as such shall sell and dispose of them as Their Highnesses may command. And we shall take your goods, and shall do you all the mischief and damage that we can, as to vassals who do not obey and refuse to receive their lord and resist and contradict him.

Now I'm getting angry, as well as feeling sad. I can't believe that something so appalling and spiritually corrupt was at the base of the European "invasion," as you call it. Why didn't anyone object? Weren't there at least a few good priests who put up a fuss?

Yes, there were some, Grandson. There are always good people of conscience. But do not forget how dangerous any opposition would have been. Maybe that is why I have found precious few accounts of what you might call religious dissidents who risked their lives by speaking out.

Who were they, and what did they say? What did they do?

In Santo Domingo, in a little makeshift church with a thatched roof, Father Antonio de Montesinos spoke the following words to his congregation of Spaniards in 1511:

> Tell me by what right, by what law do you keep these Indians in such cruel, such horrible bondage? By what authority have you waged such detestable wars against these peoples, who lived quietly and peacefully on land that was their own? Wars in which you destroyed incalculable numbers of them by homicide and slaughters surpassing anything in history? Why do you keep them so oppressed and exhausted, not giving them enough to eat, not curing the illnesses they develop from the excessive labor you force upon them, so that they pass away— no you murder them!—in order to extract and obtain gold every single day? . . . Are you not bound to love them as yourselves? Why can't you comprehend this? Why are you lost in this deep lethargic sleep? Rest assured, in this state you can no more be saved than the Moors or Turks, who do not have faith in Jesus Christ and do not desire it.

This same sermon could have been preached for the next 500 years and could still be preached to the men and women who govern your country today. Be certain, Grandson, that I am talking of those forefathers and their descendants that your people consider among the finest—the Endicotts, the Winthrops, Washington, Jefferson, the Adams family, Madison, Monroe, Jackson, Clay, Calhoun, and the Roosevelts, to name a few. To my people, Mount Rushmore is an abomination and a monument to spiritual malaise. It would be like erecting a monument to Hitler in Jerusalem.

I will not mention those of your political leaders who are still alive and in office, for they might yet have a change of heart before they cross over to the Spirit World, but I am not counting on it. The only real difference today is that the genocide is carried out by economic, legal, and cultural means, though there has been plenty of outright murder, especially in Central and South America in recent times, and even on the reservations in this country. And believe me, Grandson, the United States government has been involved, and continues to be involved, in these atrocities. Our elders consider all Indians political prisoners of your government.

But, let us continue with the historical development. Are you still with me?

I am, Grandfather. But aren't you tired? Would you like some lunch now? I'll fix up one of my specialties—grilled cheese sandwiches. Tommy and I brought up a wonderful block of cheddar cheese.

Chasing Deer: Thank you for the lunch, Grandson. I am refreshed now and ready to continue, but first let us purify ourselves with sage, cedar, and sweetgrass, to send away the spirits of those who were murdered and who have been drawn to us by our conversation.

John: I do feel better now, Grandfather. More clear and peaceful.

So, Grandson, in the year 1500, Bartholemew Las Casas came to the Caribbean with Columbus, and in 1510 he became the first Catholic priest to be ordained in the New World. Fortunately for future historians, he chronicled much of the Spanish genocide. We are greatly indebted to him, as much of this history was unknown until his book was published in 1875. He wrote: "I am recording what I have seen with my own eyes over a period of fifty years, a candid account intended for posterity." A few passages, from the hundreds available, will show you the mercilessness and brutality of the European invaders.

According to Father Las Casas, the Spaniards "tore babies from their mother's breast by their feet, and dashed their heads against the rocks. . . ." The Spaniards found pleasure in inventing all kinds of odd cruelties, the more cruel the better, with which to spill human blood. They built a long gibbet, low enough for the toes to touch the ground and prevent strangling, and hanged 13 at a time in honor of Christ Our Saviour and the 12 Apostles.

While hanging, the Indians were disemboweled and then, for good measure, while still alive, they were wrapped in straw and burned. Once the gibbet was clear, they could begin again. Of the extent of the genocide, Las Casas left no doubt. He wrote, "While I was in Cuba, 7,000 babies died in three months." In Hispañola alone, the native population dropped from about eight million in 1496 to less than twenty thousand by 1518. In Central America, Pedro de Alvarado and his compatriots, who came after Columbus, "killed more than four or five million people in fifteen or sixteen years, from the year 1525 to 1540, and they continue to kill and destroy those who are still left, and so they will kill the remainder."

Finally, a report from some concerned Dominican friars contains the following: "Some Christians encountered an Indian woman, who was carrying in her arms a child at suck; and since the dog they had with them was hungry they tore the child from the mother's arms and flung it still living to the dog, who proceeded to devour it before the mother's eyes."

I can't begin to imagine how people could harden their hearts like that. How could anyone feed a baby to a dog, or mutilate and torture people in the name of Christ and the Apostles? I know that vengeance is a dangerous emotion, Grandfather, because it gives rise to more violence. But right now, that's exactly what I feel.

Vengeance is only bad if you act upon it rashly, Grandson. Let it stay for a while; do not chase it away. In a good heart like yours, it will convert by itself into the intention to create a more loving world, and perhaps it will even show you the way to do that. Father Las Casas must have felt much the same as you do. He concludes:

> The Spaniards boldly entered this New World, a land that was unknown in past centuries. Once here, they disobeyed their Lord and committed enormous and extraordinary crimes: they massacred uncounted thousands of Indians, scattered their flocks, burned their villages, razed their cities; without any justification, the Spaniards did horrible and shameful things to a suffering people. Fierce, rapacious, and cruel, could the Spaniards have had any knowledge of the one true God revealed to the Indians by our priests?

His accounts sound more like something you'd expect from barbarians like Genghis Khan or Tamerlane—not from a Christian nation like Spain. Surely this was some aberration, Grandfather.

Unfortunately, it was not. Spain and other European-Christian nation/states had been using the same tactics since their founding several centuries earlier. Just think about the Crusades. They set the precedent for what was to happen in the Americas. I will read you what Francis Jennings, the American historian, has to say on the matter. He is better at following the logic of the marriage of Church and State than I am. This connection between religion and destruction is so foreign to our native way of thinking.

Jennings writes:

> The Crusades had well established the principle that war conducted in the interests of the Holy Church was automatically just. . . . The crusading mentality was formed by the feudal warlords' urge to conquest; in its turn it found the rational-

ization for conquest and imprinted itself on everything the conquerors would do or become. The invaders of strange continents assumed an innate and absolute superiority over all other peoples because of divine endowment; their descendants would eventually secularize the endowment to claim it from nature instead of God, but would leave its absolute and innate qualities unchanged. And, their enemies were also the enemies of the Crusader's god and therefore outside the protection of the moral law applicable to god's devotees. No slaughter was impermissible, no lies dishonorable, no breach of trust shameful, if it advantaged the champions of true religion. In the gradual transition from religious conception to racial conception, the gulf between persons calling themselves Christian and other persons, whom they called heathen, translated smoothly into a chasm between whites and coloreds.

I guess Bob Dylan had this kind of thing in mind when he wrote "With God on Our Side." I know that more people have been killed in the name of religion than anything else. It almost makes me embarrassed to be a Christian. But I am terribly bothered at the thought that this country, which I've been raised to serve, was founded on just that kind of thinking and atrocious behavior.

You are right to be bothered by the realization that many of your leaders were willing conspirators in genocide, hungering more for power than for justice. But one should never be embarrassed by one's spiritual beliefs. Surely Jesus could not be happy with what has been done in his name. Our people have always been taken by your Jesus, if not by your churches. Certainly you see that the oppressors were Christian in name only. One has only to look at the history of the Western world to see that power, money, and conquest have mattered much more than the true spiritual life that, no matter what one's religion is, is always based on respect and love.

Tell me, did things improve with the coming of the English and the French to the coast of North America?

Unfortunately, Grandson, whether it was Dutch, English, or French invaders, the story was the same wherever they landed. The slaughter continued. Tribe after tribe was decimated. In the East, in less than a half-century's contact, there was a 98 percent decrease in the Abenaki; a 92 percent decrease in the Mohicans, and a 95 percent decline in the Quiripi-Unquachog. The attrition rate was similar for other tribes, and the 67 percent genocide of the Maliseet-Passmaquoddy is the lowest I know of. To show the magnitude of the slaughter, if 67 percent of Americans were killed today, that would amount to about 175 million people.

That kind of loss would destroy our country in nothing flat. We would starve, plagues would probably break out, and there would be general turmoil.

That is exactly what happened to our people. Just imagine a decline of 95 percent, an all-too-common event for many tribes. That would leave the United States with only about 13 million people. Good-bye, culture; good-bye, economic system; good-bye to your whole standard of living.

That's almost beyond comprehension. Probably more people would survive a nuclear attack than that.

Quite so, Grandson. The blanket of blood eventually covered the entire continent, cheered on, supported, and justified by many of the prominent religious, political, and civic leaders of the day and at times carried out directly by them as in the case of the Reverend John Chivington at Sand Creek, Colorado. He stated his intentions in a speech that detailed his objective to "kill and scalp all, little and big."

Chivington attacked a village of peaceful Cheyennes and Arapahos, killing almost all of them. Before the massacre, he had been told by government officials that Black Kettle's band at Sand Creek was both unarmed and harmless, being in essence prisoners of war. But this had no effect on his decision to eliminate the defenseless people, for as he had said in response to being informed of the government's position: "Well, I long to be wading in gore." The results of his brutality can best be summarized by the testimony of the men who were there.

I will read you a few, but as I told you earlier, for every passage I read you there are hundreds more. These testimonies, and all the others, are not a few isolated renderings by a small minority of disaffected people. The original sources of American history are filled with descriptions of genocide, fear, greed, and hatred. I will have accomplished my task if I spur you on to read more of the "forgotten" history of your people. When our prophecies come true, as they are beginning to, I want nothing more than for you to be able to help lead your people out of the chaos and destruction that lack of a true spiritual life has created.

So here we go—the reports of witnesses at Sand Creek: "I saw some Indians that had been scalped, and the ears cut off the body of White Antelope," said Captain L. Wilson of the first Colorado Cavalry. "One Indian who had been scalped had also his skull smashed in, and I heard that the privates of White Antelope had been cut off to make a tobacco bag out of. I heard some of the men say that the privates of one of the squaws had been cut out and put on a stick."

John S. Smith, who was an interpreter for Chivington, recorded the following:

> All manner of depredations were inflicted on their persons;
> they were scalped, their brains knocked out; the men used their
> knives, ripped open women, clubbed little children, knocked

them in the head with their guns, beat their brains out, mutilated their bodies in every sense of the word . . . worse mutilation than any I ever saw before, the women all cut to pieces . . . children two or three months old; all ages lying there.

I will spare you any more horrific detail except to tell you that Lt. James D. Cannon recorded that he did not see a man, woman, or child who had not been scalped and mutilated; and many in the ranks of Chivington's soldiers had the genitals of the Indian women stretched over their saddle horns and over their hats. To add a macabre footnote, many upstanding Christian citizens of the West sent scalps back East to their family and friends as souvenirs.

Wasn't there any code of honor, no sparing of the defenseless, of women and children? Was Chivington punished?

Sand Creek was one of the few Indian massacres that prompted a congressional investigation. The public was invited to the Denver Opera House to discuss the massacre. But when the question was raised as to whether it would be better to try to "civilize" the Indians rather than to exterminate them, the unanimous outcry was for their death. One senator wrote to a friend, "There suddenly arose such a shout as is never heard unless upon some battlefield—a shout almost loud enough to raise the roof of the opera house—'EXTERMINATE THEM EXTERMINATE THEM.'" Nothing, of course, happened to Chivington.

When Europeans arrived on this continent, it was always described as a great wilderness despite the fact that millions of people lived here for tens of thousands of years. The reason for coming to America is usually described as the search for religious tolerance and freedom. And perhaps that was the truth for some settlers. But for the majority, the real reason for immigration was the search for wealth.

Despite the fact that our people had been here for thousands of years, the Europeans did not see us as "owners" of our land for the simple reason that according to the thinking of international law at the time, only those people who were settled in one place could claim ownership. This was despite the fact that, as even Captain John Smith noted when he cataloged Indian lands, every chief knew the boundaries of his land as did the tribe in general. Your people saw us as wandering nomads, but we knew perfectly well where our land ended and another's began.

But, as your generation says, what goes around comes around. I think that is the Buddhist definition of karma, is that right? One of our prophets said that while the White man was the last to come to our land, he shall be here for the shortest time. And, of course, your fate is intimately bound to the rest of humanity, including that of the Red people.

All you have told me leaves me filled with doubt about the very foundations and institutions of Western culture. After all, the real test of any culture, religion, or institution is what it produces in terms of the humanity and decency of its people. The scorecard looks pretty dismal for my culture, Grandfather. I certainly would not want to face my Creator, having knowingly participated in the kinds of things that you have described to me.

It depends on the kind of Maker you believe in, John. The Reverend Cotton Mather believed that the Indians were the devil's people. Old Satan himself, according to Mather, had planted the Indian peoples in such a remote and faraway land "in hopes that the gospel of the Lord Jesus Christ would never come here to destroy or disturb his absolute empire over them." I think that an Indian of the time might have thought that the Great Creator, in his mercy, placed his people where he did to keep them as far away as possible from the degenerate influence of the devilish European!

Now, as warfare and epidemics spread through the Indian nations, it pleased the good Christians to no end, for as the Reverend William Hubbard explained, "Civilization was the property of the divinely chosen people of New England." And Massachusetts Governor William Bradford wrote, "It pleased God to visit these Indians with a great sickness though in this regard God was not perfect for 50 of every thousand Indians survived."

Nonetheless, Bradford had to conclude that even an annihilation of 95 percent of them warranted gratitude and thanks to the Almighty "for the marvelous goodness and providence of God."

Cotton Mather agreed, so both the religious and the secular were joined in their exaltation "that the Woods were almost cleared of these pernicious Creatures, to make room for a better growth." Somewhat later, Mather wrote, "Once you have got the Track of those Ravenous howling Wolves, then pursue them vigorously; turn not back till they are consumed. . . . Beat them small as the Dust before the Wind."

In 1703, another New England religious leader, Solomon Stoddard, proposed to the governor of Massachusetts that resources be given to the godly citizens of the land to hunt the Indians as one would bears or wolves, using dogs. In Stoddard's own words, "The dogs would be an extreme terror to the Indians. . . . Dogs would do a great deal of execution upon the enemy and catch many an Indian too light on foot for us."

Reverend Stoddard was as good at rationalization and justification as he was at genocide for "if the Indians were as other people . . . it might be looked upon as inhumane to pursue them in such a manner." Lastly, when the massacres were over, the remaining captured Indians were either sold into slavery or given to the gentry for servants. Indeed, the eminent founding father, John Endicott of Massachusetts, and his pastor, Hugh Peter, wrote Governor Winthrop with a request for Indian slaves.

While most people in this country only associate slavery with the Black people, it was a common fate for the Red people, also.

By the latter part of the 17th century, the vast majority of Virginia's Indians had been killed, so plans were being made to make their subjugation through murder and slavery complete. In his fine book, *American Holocaust,* historian David E. Stannard tells us what happened:

> In time, a combination plan of genocide and enslavement, as initially proposed by the colony's Governor William Berkeley, appeared to quiet what had become a lingering controversy over whether it was best to kill all the Indians or to capture them and put them to forced labor: Berkeley's plan was to slaughter all the adult Indian males in a particular locale, "but to spare the woman and children and sell them," says Edmund Morgan. This way the war of extermination "would pay for itself," since it was likely that a sufficient number of female and child slaves would be captured "to defray the whole cost."

Ironically enough, at least from my perspective, when the patent was given to the founders of the Massachusetts Bay Colony by the English Crown, it read, in part, that "the Principall Ende of this Plantation was to wynn and incite the Natives of [the] Country, to the Knowledge and Obedience of the onlie true God and Savior of Mankinde and the Christian Fayth." That was in 1629, and yet 13 years later, Thomas Lechford could write that "there hath not been sent forth by any Church to learn the Native's language, or to instruct them in Religion." Four years later, the first Massachusetts missionary to the Indians, John Eliot, finally preached to them.

Given the treatment that the Indians had received up until that time, it is no wonder that they had no desire to listen to anything Eliot had to say. This poor reception by the Indians of "the Word" of God infuriated the magistrates of the colonies. The result was a proclamation that the government had jurisdiction over the Indians, so they promptly drafted a law for the suppression of native religions. The law also established missionary reservations for the Indians who were converted to Christianity. The Court decreed "that no Indian shall at any time pawwaw, or perform outward worship to their false gods, or to the devill [sic]." Indians found practicing their own religion were subject to the "penalty of heavy fines." So much for the myth of the United States as a haven for religious freedom.

Wait a minute, now, Grandfather, the Puritans supposedly fled to America from England via Holland to escape religious intolerance and persecution. Are you are telling me that as soon as they got here, they did the same thing to the Indians?

That is exactly what happened, Grandson.

Didn't any of the clergy or the court appreciate the duplicity of their behavior? Of course, what you're telling me happened before the actual founding of the United States, but surely the seeds of religious freedom, which became law in our Constitution, didn't just spring up in 1776 or at the Constitutional Convention a few years later.

If there was any light in Puritan New England, it was the Reverend Roger Williams. Williams was viewed as a religious heretic and had been banned from Massachusetts. In 1636 he set up his own Providence Colony in what is now Rhode Island. While Williams also saw the Red people as devil worshipers, he still dealt with us decently and as human beings with rights. In fact, a lot of the friction with the Massachusetts Puritans that led to his banishment was due to his insistence that the land belonged to the Indians and that the English had no right to take it. Williams spoke out and said that if they wanted Indian land, they had to purchase it, just as they would have had to do if they wanted a White man's land. But that was not the position of the political and religious leaders of the day.

The vast majority believed, as did Reverend Increase Mather, "that the Lord God our Father hath given us for a rightful possession the land of the Heathen amongst whom we live." And the military leaders carried out with haste and, I am sorry to say, with evident joy, the wishes of the religious and political leaders. After attacking a village of about 400 sleeping Pequots, one of the leaders of the raid, Captain John Mason, boastfully said, "God laughed his Enemies and the Enemies of the People to Scorn, making them as a fiery Oven. . . .Thus did the Lord Judge among the Heathen, filling the Place with dead Bodies." And his co-leader, Captain John Underhill, justified the slaughter because "we had sufficient light from the word of God for our proceedings."

As the disgraceful terrorization of the Indians continued, Williams wrote the General Court of Massachusetts on October 5, 1654, to raise a voice of conscience against the genocide. In one letter he writes:

> Are not the English of this land, generally, a persecuted people from their native soil? And hath not the God of peace and Father of mercies made these natives more friends in this, than our native countrymen in our own land to us? Have they not entered leagues of love, and to this day continue peaceable commerce with us? Upon which I humbly ask, how it can suit with Christian ingenuity to take hold of some seeming occasions for their destruction?

Williams and his followers actually purchased their land from the Narragansetts. They did not steal it.

If I remember correctly, wasn't Roger Williams's colony set up according to the twin principles of religious freedom and tolerance?

Yes, it was. As I told you, Grandson, it was Williams's strong belief that the government had no business interfering with a person's religious beliefs that got him in trouble with the Puritans. He was, we could say, America's first white liberal. Grandson, it is about time now that we leave the history of New England. I have spent so much time on the early contact between the Europeans and the Indians because it sets the stage for everything else that followed, right up to the present. The same atrocities were repeated over and over again during the relentless move of the settlers from the East Coast to the Pacific. Only the actors in the merciless passion play, and the tribes that were exterminated, change.

Here, in a nutshell, is a summary for you of the unethical and illegal means by which our land was stolen from us across your nation. As was common with the Puritans of New England, the settlers often justified what they did through Scripture. Two passages that readily come to mind are Psalms 2:8, which says, "Ask of me, and I shall give thee the heathen for thy inheritance, and the uttermost parts of the Earth for thy possession"; and Romans 13:2, "Whosoever therefore resisteth the Power, resisteth the Ordinance of God, and they that resist, receive to themselves damnation."

Now, as historian Francis Jennings has pointed out, there were five main methods by which Indian land was stolen. First of all, if an Indian happened to shoot any livestock that roamed onto their land, no matter what harm it might be causing, the Indian was hauled into court and fined. The magistrates had the authority to "order satisfaction according to law and justice." Often the "satisfaction" was their land. But, naturally, there were no penalties if an Englishman's livestock roamed on to another Englishman's land. Next, there was the nefarious use of the scourge of my people, alcohol. It was common to get an Indian drunk and then have them sign something that they could neither read nor understand. These documents invariably held up in court.

Another method, which was also usually aided by alcohol,

was to get an Indian who had no tribal authority to sell land as a supposed representative of his tribe. Again, these cases stood up in court. A fourth method was to enact fines for petty offenses for Indians, but not for Englishmen, and then foreclose on Indian lands when the fines were not paid. Last, there was simple and brutal violence.

The early Europeans may have been one thing, but surely the Founding Fathers of the United States were another.

I wish it were so, Grandson. But, it is not as you would have it, or as you have been taught. In 1779, George Washington sent orders to General John Sullivan concerning the need to attack and destroy the six Iroquois nations. I will read you part of Washington's orders to Sullivan:

> The immediate objects are the total destruction and devastation of their settlements, and the capture of as many prisoners of every age and sex as possible . . . parties should be detached to lay waste all settlements around . . . that the country may not be merely overrun, but destroyed.

Being a good soldier, Sullivan did as he was ordered and then some, writing back to Washington that there was nothing left but a "scene of drear and sickening desolation." Not surprisingly, Washington's name among the Iroquois was "Town Destroyer."

Washington was also an advocate of germ warfare, first introduced by Sir Jeffrey Amherst after whom the town of Amherst, Massachusetts, and Amherst College are named. The idea of germ warfare with smallpox was suggested by Sir Jeffrey to Colonel Henry Bouquet, after which Colonel Bouquet wrote back:

> I will try to inoculate the [Indians] with some blankets that may fall in their hands, and take care not to get the disease

myself. As it is a pity to expose good men against them, I wish we could make use of the Spanish method, to hunt them with English dogs, supported by rangers and some light horse, who would, I think, effectually extirpate or remove the vermin.

About 60 years later, Andrew Jackson took Colonel Bouquet's advice in his war against the Seminoles.

Despite the brutality of the fledgling United States government, many Indian nations continued to extend kindness and aid. During the American army's struggle for survival at Valley Forge, Chief Shenandoah of the Oneida (one of the six Iroquois Nations raided by Sullivan) sent over 700 bushels of corn from southern New York and northern Pennsylvania to help save Washington's men. Obviously, Washington had no gratitude and simply continued his extermination program.

Thomas Jefferson's treatment of the Indians was no better. In a letter to the Secretary of War in 1807, Jefferson made it clear that any tribe that interfered with the expansion of the White people westward was to be dealt with violently. He wrote: ". . .if ever we are constrained to lift the hatchet against any tribe, we will never lay it down till that tribe is exterminated, or is driven beyond the Mississippi . . . we shall destroy them all." Jefferson was true to his word. Six years later, he claimed that the United States government was left with no choice but "to pursue [the Indians] to extermination."

For the student of history, Jefferson's deceit is obvious. In November of 1802, he wrote to the Seneca chief, Handsome Lake, who was fearful of more Iroquois land being taken:

> You remind me, brother, of what I said to you when you visited me last winter, that the lands you then held would remain yours, and shall never go from you but when you should be disposed to sell. This I now repeat and will ever abide by. We, indeed, are always ready to buy land; but we will never ask, but when you wish to sell. . . .

Less than two months later, Jefferson began to outline his plan to steal those very Indian lands. The plan was simple: get them used to European trade goods, let them build up debt at the trading posts, and then take the land in payment by negotiating with their chiefs. But Jefferson was not without conscience or awareness of the genocide that he and his fellow Americans endorsed and carried out. He wrote, "I tremble for my country when I reflect that God is just."

Perhaps the most despicable of the American presidents was Andrew Jackson as he carried his country's legacy of genocide and removal of the Indians from their lands throughout the Southeast. Jackson led illegal wars, publicly fostered a policy of extermination and later removal, defied the Supreme Court decisions of John Marshall in regard to Indian sovereignty, and personally supervised mutilation of Indian men, women, and children.

"Old Hickory" took souvenirs from the corpses of the Indians he killed to send to the "ladies of Tennessee." He had the noses of those he killed cut off so that he could keep a count of his dead, and even had the flesh stripped from the massacred in order to make belts and reins for his men. At one point, he boastfully exclaimed, "I have on all occasions preserved the scalps of my killed."

When the great Seminole chief and warrior, Osceola, came forth under the white flag of truce to negotiate peace and the release of prisoners, soldiers ambushed the entire unarmed delegation of 116 men and 82 women and children. They were chained and imprisoned in St. Augustine, Florida, and later removed to Fort Moultrie, South Carolina, where Osceola died. Shortly after his burial, he was exhumed and his head cut off and sent to the Stuyvesant Institute in New York City for public display.

Jackson's wrath against the Seminoles was all the greater because, like many tribes, they gave refuge to Black slaves. When the conflagrations and murders were over, Jackson once again expressed his joy in Biblical terms. He wrote to his wife Rachel:

The hand of heaven has been pointed against the exciters
of this war, every principle [sic] villain has been either killed or
taken. . . . I think that I may say that the Indian war is at an end
for the present, the enemy is scattered over the whole face of
the Earth, and at least one half must starve and die with disease.

It would have been more honest and accurate if Jackson had
written about the "hand of Hell." Tell me, Grandson, why do you
think the White people so consistently invoked God as their permission to perform violent, immoral acts?

*I can't answer that question any better than you can,
Grandfather. But, I can tell you that they couldn't do it today. Too
many people would be outraged. During the Vietnam War, some
of the clergy spoke out strongly, people like William Sloan Coffin,
the chaplain of Yale, and the Berrigan brothers, who were
Catholic priests. I really think that the protest against the
Vietnam War marked a real change in consciousness for many of
the American people.*

I hope so, Grandson. But do not forget that there were many
who supported that war, once again by imagining the Vietnamese
to be an inferior race. And I still fear the worst from your politi-
cians, even the ones most beloved to your people. Theodore
Roosevelt thought that the destruction of the American Indian
was both "beneficial" and "inevitable." His racism was not even
hidden when he remarked that, "I don't go so far as to think that
the only good Indians are dead Indians, but I believe that nine out
of ten are, and I shouldn't like to inquire too closely into the case
of the tenth." Remember the Sand Creek Massacre? Roosevelt
said that it was "as righteous and beneficial a deed as ever took
place on the frontier." And to think that he was actually awarded
the Nobel Peace Prize.

Once again, Grandfather, I don't think he'd have gotten away with that behavior today. I have to believe that people are evolving out of such blatant racism.

On the surface I agree with you, Grandson. More people of goodwill are speaking out. But racism and discrimination are so rooted in your psychology, and even the kind of "scientific" studies that have tried to ascribe racial inferiority to some groups, that its effects lurk underground like a giant mycelial mat from which mushrooms inevitably pop up. You may be able to pick the individual mushrooms, but the mat remains to spawn many more.

Think about the Indian boarding schools that have broken down the families of my people and deprived our children of their culture. On the surface, these may seem a noble gesture to educate our children, but they are a subtle form of murder.

Murder, Grandfather? Don't you think that's a pretty strong statement?

It is, and it is the truth. In the book *Our Brother's Keeper,* Edgar Cahn, at the time dean of the Antioch Law School, did a superb analysis of the Bureau of Indian Affairs, or BIA. Of the educational system, he writes:

> Indian children face unremitting pressure toward submission and cultural annihilation. All who pass through the Indian educational system become casualties of education waged as war. . . . The B.I.A. educational system is not primarily an "educational system." It is best understood as a major division of the bureau's own "military-industrial complex" which wages unrelenting war upon Indian survival.

At the end of the Plains Wars, Christian missionary schools and federal institutions like the infamous Carlisle Indian School were established. At these schools, the children were taught that their culture, their religion, and their way of life were both wrong and backward. They were punished for speaking their own tongue and barred from all expressions of their culture, right down to making them cut their hair and wear White man's clothes.

Most important, the children were not allowed to practice their religion until quite recently. You may be shocked by this, Grandson, but Indian religions were illegal until Congress finally acted in 1978. Even then, our freedom of religious expression was limited, and it was further restrained a decade later by the Supreme Court. The attempt to annihilate traditional Indian culture continues today.

Let us look at what is still going on. Of the 371 treaties negotiated with the Indians since the founding of the United States, none have been kept, and they are all still being violated. About 30 percent of all Indian children are put into adoptive homes or foster care, yet only one percent are taken from their parents because of abuse. Worse yet, 85 percent end up in non-Indian homes.

In order to further destroy both the Indians and our culture, the federal government initiated a large-scale sterilization program. A Choctaw-Cherokee physician, Connie Uri, uncovered this program when she was asked by a young Indian woman for a womb transplant. She scoured the records of the BIA-run Indian Health Service Hospital in Claremont, Oklahoma, and discovered that 75 percent of the sterilizations were nontherapeutic. Many of the women did not understand the true nature of the surgery, thought it was a kind of reversible birth control, or even signed the consent forms while groggy from sedation after childbirth.

Following Dr. Uri's lead, Senator James Abourezk initiated a federal investigation by the General Accounting Office. The resulting report gave the results of a survey from four out of the twelve regions with Indian Health Services hospitals. In a three-year period, over 3,400 sterilizations were performed; 3,000 of them on Indian women under the age of 44. In not one instance were the women offered consent forms that met federal guidelines and requirements. About 5 percent of Indian women were being sterilized, Grandson, and this in a nation that you prize for its fairness and concern for human rights.

Indian women launched their own investigation of the United States government's Office of Population, headed by Dr. R. T. Ravenholt. The investigation "would uncover an international sterilization program managed in part by Dr. Ravenholt's Office of Population." Ravenholt told the Population Association of America in St. Louis that the critics were "a really radical extremist group lashing out at a responsible program so that revolution would occur."

William Byler, who conducted a long-term study of the removal of Indian children from their homes, concluded that "the main thrust of federal policy, since the close of the Indian wars, has been the breakup of the extended family and the clan structure [and] to detribalize and assimilate Indian populations." In 1968, the subcommittee for Indian education of the United States Congress heard the following: "There is not one Indian child who has not come home in shame and tears after one of those sessions in which he is taught that his people are dirty and animal-like, something less than a human being."

During the late 1960s and the early 1970s, the American Indians began protesting against the unremitting theft of their lands and resources by the federal and state governments, largely for the benefit of large industrial corporations and the United States military. This led to the rise of the American Indian Movement, or AIM, which is probably best known for its stand against the oppression and police-state tactics that were used against the Lakota Nation on the Pine Ridge Reservation.

On Pine Ridge, as on other reservations, the FBI backed, supplied, encouraged, and goaded a private police force to harass, intimidate, and murder those Indians asserting their rights and wishing to live in traditional ways. Whenever we try to climb out of the hole of alcoholism and welfare dependency that reservation life has spawned, your government is there to push us back in.

Edgar Cahn summarizes the BIA's role in Indian affairs as follows:

> Through the pervasiveness of the bureau's role, the exercise of power and administrative programs by the BIA has come to ensure that every effort by the Indians to achieve self-realization is frustrated and penalized, that the Indian is kept in a state of permanent dependency as his price of survival and that alienation from his people and his past is rewarded and encouraged.

The American Indian Movement was particularly concerned with the FBI's failure to investigate major crimes on the reservations where murder of traditional Indians trying to preserve the dignity and spirituality of the old ways, and those protesting their treatment, had become commonplace. Since the FBI was behind many of these crimes, it felt little urgency to investigate them and was sure that America's poorest population could do little to halt the violence and the cover-ups.

But the FBI underestimated the tenacity of the Indian warriors who opposed them. Let me give you a case in point, and I stress that it is far from an isolated example. In January of 1973, Wesley Bad Heart Bull was stabbed to death in a South Dakota bar by a White businessman named Darold Schmidt. Schmidt had bragged earlier that "he was going to kill him an Indian." And so he did. Several weeks later, Schmidt was arrested for second-degree manslaughter. Had he murdered a White man, the charge would surely have been more serious.

The Indians protested and asked AIM to intercede, hoping to get the charge upgraded to first-degree murder. A meeting with the local magistrates was arranged. But when the Indians arrived at the Custer County Courthouse, it was surrounded by police-men in riot gear. Nonetheless, the meeting began. Unfortunately, Wesley's mother, Sarah Bad Heart Bull, arrived late and her request to enter the courtroom was denied. A local policeman grabbed her and threw her to the ground. A ruckus ensued, and the courthouse caught fire. The result was typical of White jus-tice for the Red man—Schmidt was given two months probation, and Mrs. Bad Heart Bull was sentenced to three to five years in prison for assaulting an officer.

Between 1973 and 1976, there were over 60 political mur-ders on and around Pine Ridge Reservation. Few have been investigated, and none solved. From 1973 after Wounded Knee Two, up to 1976, the yearly murder rate on Pine Ridge was 170 per 100,000, a startling number nine times that of Detroit, America's murder capital. In a city of five million, this would have resulted in 25,500 political murders in three years.

Let me tell you just one more story about your legal system that may fuel a higher vision for you as a lawyer, Grandson. On September 5, 1975, the FBI, armed with a search warrant, invad-ed the home of the Lakota medicine carrier and spiritual leader Leonard Crow Dog. They arrived by helicopter and armored per-sonnel carriers, fully suited in paramilitary gear, during a reli-gious ceremony. The pretense was to look for weapons possibly involved in the killing of two agents some two months earlier. The actual intent was the continued persecution of traditional elders and the disruption of religious observances.

The house was ransacked and sacred objects purposely defiled. Crow Dog, fearing for the lives of his family and the oth-ers gathered at his home, picked up a rifle that he did not use and could not use offensively, as his sacred oaths forbade it. He was promptly arrested and charged with assault with a deadly weapon.

A trial carried out with the alacrity of hangings in the Old West quickly sentenced him to five years in prison. After his ini-tial incarceration, he was moved from prison to prison, since he was regarded as a hero by many of the inmates. As a result of the adulation, Crow Dog was kept mostly in solitary confinement. During the six months that he was transferred to five different prisons, he lost 50 pounds and his health began to fail.

While incarcerated in Virginia, Crow Dog was examined by a prison physician and told that the reason for his weight loss and failing health was a brain tumor. With the rise of social activism among the clergy in the 1960s, the National Council of Churches was closely monitoring Crow Dog's treatment while imprisoned. Given the handling of other Indian spiritual leaders, the Council feared for his well-being. And they were correct in their concerns. Federal officials were actually preparing to perform a lobotomy on the medicine carrier.

The National Council of Churches sent two independent physicians to examine Crow Dog. Both concluded that his failing health was due to the dire conditions of his imprisonment, including one three-week stint in a five-foot-high solitary confinement cell during which he was not allowed out to exercise. Upon reviewing his treatment, Amnesty International declared him a political prisoner. Finally, due to the efforts of Amnesty International and a vocal campaign on the part of the National Council of Churches, he was paroled on March 21, 1977.

Crow Dog's treatment makes me sick, Grandfather. I can't believe they were going to give him a lobotomy. If people of goodwill hadn't intervened, he would have been subjected to the equivalent of Nazi tactics against the Jews. And this in a democracy.

I was always taught that the FBI and the Department of Justice were the defenders of the rights of the citizens of this country. Their character and behavior are supposed to be beyond reproach. But what you have told me sounds more like something one would expect from a Latin American dictatorship.

I'm feeling so disillusioned by the behavior of people that I was raised to trust and admire—that I wanted to be one of. I still want to go into law, Grandfather, but I've known for a long time that the law itself can be corrupt, especially when it protects the interests of the powerful. My hope is that I can expose and stop that corruption and begin to make amends to your people for what was done in the past and what continues into the present.

You will not be alone, either, Grandson. The National Council of Churches has begun to speak out and accept the role of true spiritual leaders. It is a very positive change and one that I both respect and welcome, since the atrocities going on today are not limited to North America, but extend to the treatment of the indigenous peoples of Central and South America as well.

While the killing of Indians in those lands never really stopped in modern times, in the 1950s the genocide of the Indians of the deep forest began in earnest. When the atrocities came to the attention of the Brazilian government, they were quick to act and avoided any cover-up, which was a most honorable position. The majority of the perpetrators, it turned out, were in one way or another connected to the Indian Protective Services, or IPS. Though the genocide had been exposed, "it was a different matter to bring the instigators of such crime to book, for only too often they proved to be powerful, even international land speculators. It was a time, too, when multinational corporations were joining the drive to develop the untapped natural resources and to fill the apparently empty spaces of Latin America."

Once again, Grandfather, the exploitation of the land for profit is a major motivation for continuing genocide. How great that the Brazilian government was willing to admit this.

It is one thing to admit it, Grandson, and another altogether to stop it. The decreases in population that these land speculators, in partnership with certain missionary organizations, instigated over the past 25 years or so are in line with those of the Caribbean and the United States centuries earlier.

The conservative Brazilian newspaper, *O Jornal*, pointed out, "In reality, those in control of these Indian Protective Services posts [where the majority of the atrocities have taken place] are North American Missionaries—they are in all the posts—and they disfigure the original Indian culture and enforce the acceptance of Protestantism."

When *O Jornal* spoke of the disfigurement of the Indian culture, it meant the banning by missionaries of Indian ceremonies of all kinds, of native dances, of the playing of native instruments, of self-treatment by Indians using their own medicinal remedies, of self-decoration in any form, or the wearing of apparel other than of the plainest and drabbest kind.

The total number of pages needed to outline the genocide and inhuman abuse published by the Attorney General of Brazil came to 5,115. From Norman Lewis's book, *The Missionaries*, which I suggest that you read, comes a small list of newspaper headlines and statements by the Brazilian Ministry of the Interior. I will read you a few, Grandson:

> Rich landowners of the municipality of Pedro Alfonso attacked the tribe of Craos and killed about 100. The worst slaughter took place in Aripuana, where the Cintas Largas Indians were attacked from the air using sticks of dynamite. Survivors were chopped up by mercenaries employed on an overland expedition. The Maxacalis were given fire-water by the landowners who employed gunmen to shoot them down. Landowners engaged a notorious pistoleiro and his band to massacre Canelas Indians. The Nhambiquera Indians were mown down by machine-gun fire.
>
> Two tribes of Patachos were exterminated by giving them smallpox injections. In the Ministry of the Interior it was stated yesterday that crimes committed by certain ex-functionaries

of the IPS amounted to more than 1,000, ranging from tearing out Indians' finger-nails to allowing them to die without assistance. To exterminate the tribe Beicos-de-Pau, Ramis Bucair, Chief of the 6th Inspectorate, explained, an expedition was formed which went up the River Arinos carrying presents and a great quantity of foodstuffs for the Indians. These were mixed with arsenic and formicides . . . next day a great number of the Indians died, and the whites spread the rumour they had died from an epidemic.

The deluge of rain that had begun in the late afternoon, as the Thunder Beings echoed the anguish of John and Chasing Deer, continued into a night robbed of starlight. But as with the Indian people, John knew that their light was not extinguished, but only hidden temporarily by clouds.

As human beings, particularly those of us who were raised in Western culture, we always want to know why. Why have the American Indians been hunted until this day? Is it because the darkness of the oppressors feared their light? Or was it the destiny of these people, as foretold in their prophecies? If we believe the latter, then John's next conversation with Chasing Deer will reveal that our own culture is in as much danger as that of our Indian relations. But, like John, we can choose to make a difference and perhaps change the course of events before Grandmother Earth takes things into her own hands.

CHAPTER FIVE

PROPHECIES OF COMING TIMES

John awakened to the false dawn, layers of indigo clouds back-lit with streaks of pale light. An eerie luminescence turned the droplets left from the previous day's rain into pearls hanging from the limbs of the junipers outside the small living room window. He arose without thinking, led by the haunting song of a dove into the thicket of spruce trees behind Chasing Deer's cabin. Bare feet sinking into the cool carpet of pine needles, John made his way through the semi-darkness to the gnarled old tree in which the little bird perched, its black eyes intent upon the two-legged visitor.

Wrapping himself in the worn trade blanket that he had brought from the cabin, John leaned against the base of the tree and began to think about the future—not only his own, but that of the Earth. This was the day that Chasing Deer would reveal many prophecies of coming times to John, and he wanted to prepare himself.

Soon he was in the land of twilight sleep, the place of reverie, where infinite possibilities exist and time has never been. His spirit flew to the bird on the wings of his longing for a better world. *Are you a mourning dove,* wondered John, *celebrating the dawn of a new era, or are you a mourning dove whose plaintive song speaks of the death of a world that would not awaken to compassion?*

"I am what you would have me be, little brother, for what is any sign or portent but the truest measure of the human heart? Tell me, what would it mean for you to live in a new world based on respect and care? Would you continue to open the veins of Grandmother Earth and take her blood to power your machines? Would you go out to a restaurant and eat while others go hungry? What would you personally be willing to sacrifice for a new world to be born?"

"Little dove, these are difficult questions. How can I answer truly before I've thought things through? I've enjoyed living here in these woods, in the old ways. But I also enjoy my car and central heating. Do I have to give up these things, or can they be part of a new future where we can honor Grandmother Earth by harnessing the power of the waters or the winds or of Grandfather sun?"

"Listen to the Voice of The Great Mysterious, little brother, as it speaks through the great prophets of the past and calls to you from the possible futures. For what is the Creator but the force of harmony, guidance, and beauty that is forever beckoning us to bring a better world into being? The choice of futures, my two-legged relation, is always and forever yours. But remember, the future is an active choice—not just a hopeful fantasy."

The face of Grandfather Sun was beginning to peer over the horizon, turning the pearls of moisture into drops of scarlet, the blood of life, when John was aroused from his reverie by the resonant voice of Chasing Deer.

"Are you out here, Grandson? Come and honor the new day."

And so began the fourth morning of John's visit with Chasing Deer, the day when the elder would reveal stunning prophecies of possible futures—some of beauty and others that spoke of the destruction of the world. After a brisk bath in the cold stream, the two men purified themselves with fragrant sage and sweetgrass and smoked Chasing Deer's old pipe that had been lovingly beaded by his mate in red, black, yellow, and white—the colors of the four directions and of the four races of human beings.

As Chasing Deer recounted the first prophecy, the vision of His Crazy Horse who foretold a coming together of all the nations—all the four colors—under the great Tree of Peace, John kept returning to the words of the dove. *What does this prophecy mean to me personally? What am I willing to sacrifice? Knowing these things, how then shall I live?*

Ⓧ   Ⓧ   Ⓧ

John: Grandfather, you've told me prophecies about the coming of the White man and what was done to your people. They were right on the mark. And I understand from yesterday's discussion that the past has not really passed, and that your people and their wisdom are still oppressed and denied. This morning I woke up before dawn, and I've been thinking about what personal choices I would have to make to create a different world, a better future. In fact, I was speaking to a little dove about it, if you can believe that.

Chasing Deer: I better send you back to civilization soon, Grandson, for you are turning into an Indian! No White woman will want you—talking to trees and birds, and bathing naked in icy streams. But you know that I am kidding with you, Grandson. Of what did you and the winged one speak?

About what you just said, Grandfather. How can I go back and live in my culture like nothing has changed when my understanding of life is totally different? If I want to live in a world where the idea of "all my relations" is a reality, not just a noble sentiment, then I have to make my life consistent with that belief. That's going to require some changes. And the way I choose to live may seem strange to other people. Maybe you're right—no woman will want me.

You are very earnest, Grandson, and I admire that. But like the newly converted, you tend to want instant answers. Keep your heart pure, your intention focused, and the right road will reveal itself to you. Take it easy, Grandson. Learn to trust yourself and see where it leads. By this, I do not mean to become lazy or to lose your discrimination, but to wait a little and listen to your heart. And as for women, you will be drawn to one whose heart resonates with your own, of this I am certain.

Well, that's a hopeful prophecy, Grandfather. Got any more like that?

There are many hopeful prophecies, Grandson. And as the dove foretold, each one asks us to think about what they mean personally in our own lives, choices, and behavior. For now try to let go of that larger question because we will talk of it in the days to come. Today, just listen to The Great Mysterious as it has spoken, and continues to speak, through the prophecies of my people. Have you ever heard of the great visionary and warrior His Crazy Horse?

I'm not sure, Grandfather. I think I remember hearing of a Crazy Horse. Is that the same person?

It surely is, Grandson. When the names of my people get recorded by the Whites, sometimes only part of the name is used, or it may even be changed. Now, His Crazy Horse was of my father's people, the Oglala Lakota. Settle back and be comfortable, because I am going to tell you his prophecy in the context of his life and what was happening to his people at that time. It is a long and interesting story.

In the year of 1871, during the early part of the Moon of Making Fat, what you would call June, His Crazy Horse was ill at ease. Yet it was a time of peace with the Whites, a time of bounty and, for a while still, life was able to be lived much as the

Lakota had for thousands of years. His home life with his wife Black Shawl was a source of great comfort and happiness. All was well, and with the coming of his daughter, They Are Afraid of Her, His Crazy Horse had become a doting father. He loved to make his girl child giggle, tickling her with a rabbit's tail and shaking her antelope hoof rattle. As she grew older, they played together with her favorite toys, a willow hoop painted in beautiful colors and a bouncing buffalo bladder filled with stones.

Even though the Lakota had suffered great losses through warfare and dislocation, they still lived according to the old ways in this period of temporary peace. There was time for hunting, dancing, ceremonies, and an occasional raid to steal some horses from the Crows. In 1868, Red Cloud had signed the Fort Laramie Treaty, but only after the Bozeman Trail forts were abandoned and the White soldiers had finally fled after Red Cloud had burned Forts Smith, Reno, and Kearny to the ground. It was the first war that the United States had lost, and to what General Miles had called "the best cavalry soldiers on Earth," the Lakota.

According to the treaty, all of South Dakota west of the Missouri, including the sacred Black Hills, was ceded to the Lakota "for as long as the rivers shall run and the grass shall grow." The fertile hunting grounds of the Powder River area were also named "unceded Indian territory." This land ran from west of the Black Hills, north of the Platte River, to as far west as the summits of the Bighorn Mountains. At last the Lakota believed that they would be left alone by the rapacious White man. But His Crazy Horse was troubled. When had White men ever kept a promise?

His Crazy Horse's anxious mind was swimming with questions. His heart told him that although things were peaceful now, the pale, hairy people would continue to come to the lands of the Lakota no matter what the treaties said. His previous experience with the settlers and their army told him that they spoke words with a deceitful heart. Did they have no Grandfathers and

Grandmothers to teach them? Was there no love between parents and children? What else could make them so shameless, so devoid of any sense of place, of any sense of honor? Who were these people, and why did the blood flow like ice in his heart at the thought of them? Each unanswerable question only raised more concerns.

Why did these people invade Indian land in the first place, and where did they come from? From the East, that is all he knew. Why did they place the things of the world before the Creator? Why did they not honor The Great Mysterious that binds all together? Strangely enough, they even feared death. Did they have no respect for the wisdom of Grandmother Earth and the Creator? Did they not see the seasons change or gaze at the sun rising and setting? They have eyes, he lamented, but they cannot see. The more His Crazy Horse thought, the more he found these people bewildering and lacking in humanity, and that was what made them so frightening. They were deaf to the Creator's Instructions.

Why did they ceaselessly search for the yellow stones (gold) of Grandmother as if crazed and possessed? Why did they kill women and children even when peace had been made with them as they did to Black Kettle's People at Sand Creek? What manner of men, so lacking in manhood, would senselessly accept and follow orders from another to kill and maim? These were not men at all. So how can one deal with people so devoid of Spirit, so full of lies and hate? They must be stopped. But how?

His Crazy Horse was not about to allow his People to be herded onto a reservation as had happened to so many other tribes, even the nearby Santee Lakota. He had seen the devastating effects of reservation life. The Ioway, the Sac and Fox, the Potawatomis, the Mandans, and others were hardly Indians any longer. They had become prisoners of the White man, begging for food, wearing his clothing, being told that their sacred ways were wrong, and being forced to worship the Christian God, the very one whom the *Wasi'chu* (a disparaging Lakota word for the White man, meaning "greedy ones") prayed to for the destruction of the Indian People. No, death was preferable. The White man's way was a fate to be avoided at any cost.

His Crazy Horse wondered how he was to protect the People. He decided to go to Bear Butte, the People's sacred mountain, for a *hanblecheyapi*, or to cry for a vision.

Now, John, the vision quest, as it is sometimes called by your people, is a most serious matter requiring purification ceremonies and a complete submission of the ego. Let me read you a fine description of this ceremony from a book called *The Wolves of Heaven:*

> It rather represented a formal submission to the spiritual powers of the universe, a readiness to accept the solidarity of life and the solidarity of physical death, an opening of the self to . . . cosmic power, and to the entering of out-of-body spirit selves. . . . It also meant a self-purification, not as a suppression of the individual but as a freeing of the individual from materialistic and immature restraints initiating a sharing of the mysterious and beautiful physical and spiritual workings of the world.

That Scheiser is a good writer, I think. He captured the true spirit of crying for a vision during which one's full attention and purity of heart must be on *Wakan Tanka* and *Tunkashila*, The Great Mysterious and Grandfather. Self-importance and self-concern are stripped away so that the supplicant can focus only on the People and how to serve them. It is a most sacred ceremony and can be done only with proper preparation and the complete absence of vainglory.

His Crazy Horse remembered the words of his father, the medicine carrier, Worm—a name he had taken after giving his son his own name, His Crazy Horse—for bravery in battle:

> Be humble as the Earth before all things, and when you
> have left the voices the body listens to, let the Spirit of Being
> flow into you until the secret Voice whispers to you through the
> needles of the pines the meaning of your life and what is to be.

So, His Crazy Horse traveled to Bear Butte with these things on his mind, a troubled man and a guardian of the People. Upon arriving at Bear Butte, he secured his horse and began his ascent to the very summit, a feat that few had dared. He carried with him only a few things: the flags of the Four Directions, his sacred pipe and tobacco of kinnikinnick and red willow, a buffalo robe, some sage, and a little food for the spirits. From the summit of Bear Butte, a beautiful and glorious world could be seen teeming with life as Grandmother Earth and *Tunkashila* would have it. The clear blue sky met the luxuriant green of the grassy plains, and the great circles of heaven and Earth were complete.

His Crazy Horse made a sacred circle with his tobacco. He covered the inside of the circle with sage and placed the flags of the Four Directions in their respective places: black to the West, white to the North, yellow to the East, and red to the South. He left his breechcloth and the food that he had brought for the spirits outside the sacred circle, carrying only his buffalo robe, his sacred pipe, and tobacco inside with him.

When all had been accomplished in a sacred way, he began his supplication: *Wakan Tanka onshimala ye oyate wani wachin cha* (Great Mysterious, have pity on me that my people may live). He then prayed the same sacred prayer to each of the seven directions: West, North, East, South, Grandmother Earth, Grandfather Sky, and *Wakan Tanka*; and, lastly, to the great circle of the universe and his connected self, ending with *Mitakuye Oyasin*—we are all related. To each of the directions he added a special prayer, each different but with a central intention: What *should* he and *could* he do for his People?

As His Crazy Horse was about to begin anew with his

prayers, he hesitated, crying to *Wakan Tanka* from deep within his spirit, that while he had cried to the Seven Directions, to the Seven Sacred Circles, what were the circles to come, the two remaining circles that remained unspoken? This broke with all tradition, and he knew it. But his heart was crying to see beyond. The Great Hoop of the People was being torn and shredded by their encounters with the White man. He knew that these were desperate times. Again, he prayed to the Seven Directions, ending with The Great Mysterious. And, again, with great courage and confidence, he asked about the circles to follow.

His Crazy Horse continued with his Seven Directions prayers until the sun set and the cool air of Bear Butte began to envelop him. He wrapped himself in his buffalo robe and lay upon the sage to rest. Periodically, he would arise and repeat his prayers. In this manner, His Crazy Horse spent his first day upon Bear Butte crying for a vision with a heavy heart for his People.

At sunrise, with the brilliant colors of life surrounding him and the sun's light circling the Earth, he knew that *Wakan Tanka* was speaking to him. He waited. He prayed with a deep intensity as all the circles of the Earth and the Sky were pulsating in the very core of his being. His hunger and thirst fled. Thus he continued until most of the third day had passed, when a great thunderstorm arose out of the West. The lightning and the hail crashed around him, but he remained untouched and unharmed. Though the Thunder Beings surrounded him, he was deeply at peace.

His Crazy Horse awakened to a brilliant morning with the sun seeming especially and remarkably intense and brilliant. A sparrow hawk circled close above him and spoke to him in a way that was clear and unmistakable. At the hawk's direction, he arose and stood upon Bear Butte to receive one of the greatest visions of the future ever entrusted to his People.

His eyes had become like the hawk's, and he could see distinctly for what seemed forever across the plains. At first his eyes were directed to a small village of Whites. They were, as usual, hectically carrying out their daily chores. His heart ached when he saw his own people living in rundown shacks on the outskirts of the White man's village, hungry and dispirited.

His far-seeing vision scanned the scene before him. Things only got worse. He saw two Indians lying torpidly in a large puddle of water, the smell of whiskey overpowering. He saw a woman washing clothes in the manner of the White man, not with the joy of serving, but with a great weariness that seemed excruciating. His heart filled with compassion and he longed to fly down and carry the burden for her. How could this be? Spirit, the defining essence of the Indian, was gone from his People.

His Crazy Horse's heart was sore, his spirit sickened. He knew very well who had caused this—the *Wasi'chu*, the ones who took whatever they wanted, callous to any way of life but their own, leaving spirit-bereft bodies in their wake to suffer upon the bosom of Grandmother. Angered and anguished, he thought, *This cannot come to pass, this living death at the hands of the Wasi'chu.*

From the brilliant light, a voice spoke to him: "This had to be," it said. "But it will pass away, for all the people of Earth must gather together like the geese that fly together in springtime. . . . Watch now, and be alert to see!"

His Crazy Horse grew peaceful and watched as he had been instructed. He saw not only the downtrodden Indians, who through years of oppression and slaughter had lost their way, but he saw also a few old ones, those with the strength of his Grandfathers, maintaining the old ways and the connection to the spirit world. He saw their spirits deeply rooted in Grandmother Earth and Grandfather Sky. They taught the few young ones who would listen. The ways of the People were passed on by the few strong ones that remained, and a fragile cord to the past remained unbroken. His Crazy Horse felt pride and hope as he beheld these precious few.

Again he turned his far-seeing gaze to the boundless prairies.

They were no longer the same. Much of the golden and green hair of Grandmother was gone. There were strange black ribbons going in every direction that had not been there before. As his vision intensified, he saw small bugs upon the black ribbons moving at great speeds. *What could this be?* His Crazy Horse wondered to himself. The bugs even carried people, and, to his amazement, some were even Lakota.

Soon a great darkness spread over the Earth. He could hear the agonies of war, see the pain and suffering in the faces of people all over the world as young men died in a far-reaching battle. Some of these young men, too, were Lakota. Yes, the young men of Earth were fighting each other, and their families wept as they were killed and wounded. When the fighting was over, people could be seen frantically building and building upon the Grandmother Earth. In the skies, he could see great silver birds— birds such as he had never seen before—strange new birds that even appeared to have lights at night.

The Earth was growing dark again, and soon all the young men were again at war, one that was totally beyond imagination. The noises were unnatural and deafening. He saw one large village completely disappear in a flash of fire and smoke. There was nothing left. It was just gone.

After this second great war, it seemed as though things were getting better for the Indian People. More of them were dancing and doing ceremonies; the men were singing the songs that strengthen the heart, and the women were trilling as in the old days. The strong drink and substances that deadened the spirit were being kept away. Things were better, but far from good, and there was still a strong wall between the People and the White man.

Once again, the Earth seemed to be shrouded in darkness, but this time there was a strong light slowly coming from the East and before it was the morning star appearing with nine points. His Crazy Horse knew that the points were the nine Sacred Circles, including the two that were yet to come. Out of the death and destruction that had befallen the Earth, he saw a sacred herb begin to grow and blossom. As the dawn grew to encircle the Earth, the herb grew into the sacred tree of his People. From a seemingly dead tree, new life was emerging "with the branches full of flowers and singing birds, and below the tree, spirit people and animals were dancing and singing as if they had all the joy in the world but could not contain it."

His Crazy Horse knew that this glorious world of light was the world of spirit—the real world of his People. With his far-seeing eyes, he also saw the "real" world of the *Wasi'chu*. In it the people seemed to be mired in a swamp and to be sinking in quicksand. The two worlds stood in sharp contrast: the world of spirit and the world of man-made struggle and sorrow. But some people on the Earthly plane began to see the light of the spirit world and stretched their hands, hearts, and minds toward it. Most, though, chose to remain in the quagmire.

Those few who saw the light of the new dawn began to proclaim it to the others, but most turned a deaf ear and chose to remain in their dull and morose state. It was as if they feared the light. But for those ready for the light, beauty began to replace ugliness, and joy and wonder returned to the Earth. His Crazy Horse could see their faces changing, for under the sacred tree, they danced in the light, and understanding was beginning to radiate from their beings. They were ready for the dawn of a new understanding.

The people dancing under the tree were of many kinds and many races. They were not just Red people, but Black, White, and Yellow. All kinds of people were radiating the joy that had returned to Earth. All of this His Crazy Horse could not understand, for in some sacred way they were all united though different. The differences were distinct, yet they were all part of a greater circle. This was very much like the relation of an individual Lakota to his tribe—a distinct and separate individual with an overriding concern for his People—free, yet bound to the tribe that gave him life and without which he could not live.

His Crazy Horse arose from his vision, came down from Bear Butte, and went to his father, the medicine carrier Worm, for help in understanding what he had seen, and for help in acting upon it for the good of the People. Worm counseled his son that the vision was true and would come to pass, both in the initial devastation and the final hope. Worm believed that the great Lakota warriors must continue to fight the White man until they could fight no longer—not because they could win, but because their strength and courage must be recognized to serve as a thread of remembrance for future generations.

The Lakota, said Worm, must unite the other tribes against the geographical, religious, and cultural incursions of the *Wasi'chu*. It must be shown that the White man could be overcome, even though the People would eventually be beaten down. Through a retelling of these Indian wars, the Lakota People would be remembered, and their strength and ceremonial life preserved. It is this remembrance that would help inspire those Grandmothers and Grandfathers in the vision to continue teaching the old ways to the few that would listen, keeping the tradition alive for its renewal at a later time.

Worm believed that, in the future, people of other races and cultures would come to the Indians seeking the wisdom of the People. Although he advised that his People continue to be wary of most Whites, he predicted that as time passed, some of them would begin to see the destructiveness of the *Wasi'chu's* path. A time would come, he told his son, when some would notice that they were out of balance and out of right relation with The Great Mysterious and Grandmother Earth despite their many packed houses of worship.

Worm said that those awakening ones would seek out those of our People still connected to the Great Circle of Life and still in touch with Grandmother Earth and Grandfather Sky. So the future generations must be prepared to help all people when the new dawn begins to brighten. And then the old medicine carrier reminded his son that White Buffalo Calf Woman had told the People about this renewal long ago. He instructed His Crazy Horse to teach the young and to be a strong example of Lakota manhood—not only for their time, but for the time of renewal to come.

There you have it. What do think?

What a strange and wonderful story. I remembered Crazy Horse, or as you say, His Crazy Horse, as a fierce warrior. But he was really a warrior of peace, responding to the hope of a future vision. And the detail was incredible, Grandfather. He saw highways crisscrossing the country. I guess cars would look like bugs with people in them from the perspective of a hawk. He saw the coming of the airplane, the two world wars, the dropping of the atomic bomb on Japan, and the fate of his people at the hands of the White man.

Indeed, Grandson, he was a great visionary and, to my mind, one of the most remarkable men ever to have lived. He followed his vision to the very end, won each of the 22 battles he fought with the United States Army, and was killed by the White man only because they deceived him.

But I fear I am sounding harsh to you again, Grandson. You know by now that when I say "White man," I refer to a way of life, a set of values, and a way of seeing the Earth, a way that is destructive, nonrelational, and out of balance. It is not a racial term, but a cultural and spiritual one. Many Indians are now, unfortunately, "White men," despite the fact that the federal government determines who is Indian and who is not by its "Degree of Indian Blood" formula. If they did that to the Whites and Blacks, then heaven only knows how many Blacks would be White and how many Whites would be Black, not to speak of the Yellow race! We know perfectly well who is Indian and who is not. As Chief Oren Lyons says, it is in the heart.

The way you express it, Grandfather, I'm turning into an Indian. And I'm hungry for these stories. I feel as if I'm recovering my own heritage as an American, and that gives me hope and a powerful vision for the future. If I thought that the destruction of the world was inevitable, I think I'd just give up and throw in the towel. I see many signs of a cultural renewal like His Crazy Horse prophesied.

The '60s ushered in a lot of changes, what some people like to call a transformation in consciousness. Up until then, very few people questioned authority or the government. In the '60s, campus protests were common. There were general protests against the administration, racial protests inspired by the nonviolent ethic of Martin Luther King, and, of course, a big outcry against the Vietnam War. After that came the Women's Movement, the demand for rights for the handicapped, and the Gay Rights Movement.

I'd say that people are definitely beginning to speak out against injustice and the arbitrary authority of power structures. There's also the Green Movement and a lot of environmental protest. We may be able to save Grandmother Earth yet. I suppose that all of this is in some part due to a spiritual awakening. There's a growing interest in religions and paths not normally traveled in America, such as Buddhism and other Eastern religions, not to mention the Native American's Red Road.

There's a movement toward things spiritual in general, and a search for wholeness in groups like Alcoholics Anonymous and other recovery programs. It's as if the void that so many people feel is crying out to be filled, and that the emptiness and rush of modern life is pushing more of us to seek a better and more balanced way.

Yet, on the other hand, Grandfather, there seems to be more violence, more abuse, less decency and civility, more crime, more senseless acting out by the young—a need for drugs, sex, or anything that will deaden pain or heighten the sense of being alive. It's a confusing time to me. On the one hand, there are many hopeful signs; yet on the other hand, things seem to be disintegrating faster than ever.

Many people have noticed this polarity, Grandson. Brant Secunda, the adopted Grandson of the two Huichol medicine carriers, Don Jose Masuwa and Dona Josefa Medrano, wrote:

> There are two things going on in the world now. On the one hand, you have dramatic change—people getting very seriously spiritual. A lot of people are dedicating their life now to some spiritual tradition or path. And then on the other hand, you have the lowest side—people killing each other in the cities and being totally uncaring, and all the homeless. You have two polarities. We have people who are changing fast, and then you have a lot of people who never even have a glimpse of the spiritual life.

Yes, many people are waking up. But just as many or more are still asleep. It used to be a battle between the young and the old, the so-called generation gap. Now it is a struggle between the conscious and the unconscious. And perhaps, as His Crazy Horse put it, the darkness is afraid of the light.

One place where darkness and light polarize is in government, which is a shame since it is supposed to be a source of help and betterment for people. Though I do not like to make generalizations, since there are always so many exceptions, I will do so to make a point about one of the Catch-22s that your society has created for itself. Men who desire power are generally not good men, and good men generally do not desire power. This makes it difficult to have good leadership. Real democracy like the Haudonosaunee, or Iroquois, had is really impossible in the United States. You know, of course, that much of the United States government was modeled after those "savages," don't you?

No, I didn't. Will you tell me something about that?

I will, Grandson, on another day. Let us concentrate on the prophecies today, and then we will see what they have to do with true democracy later. We were speaking of polarities. We started today with a very hopeful prophecy and a future in which the light of the spirit world will shine again, uniting people of all four colors. But now let me tell you of a prophecy that speaks of a fork in the road, one road leading to a rebirth such as His Crazy Horse foresaw, and the other to dire destruction if we do not return to right relationship with the Earth and one another soon enough.

This set of prophecies comes from the Anishinabe wampum belts, of which Grandfather William Commanda is the keeper. Grandfather Commanda is a Mamiwinini, or Algonquin, as his people have been called. He lives about 80 miles north of Ottawa, Canada, on the Maniwaki Indian Reserve. There were originally four wampum belts, but one was stolen and probably sold. Grandfather Commanda is always on the lookout for it. Imagine the treasures that it contains. The three belts that remain are very old. They date from 1400, 1600, and 1793. The only one that we need to talk about is the one from 1400 called the Seven Fires Belt.

According to the Seven Fires Belt, we are at a time when a Great Purification is near. And make no mistake, Grandson. A Purification is similar to the destruction of Sodom and Gomorrah or the cleansing of the Earth by great floods in the story of Noah and the ark. Grandfather says that the Purification will occur when about two-thirds of the aboriginal people of this continent have passed on. When the Purification is over, the "rightful occupants" of this land will again be in charge of it. Yet he stresses that there will be room for all peoples. But, as you will see, the Purification can be averted.

The prophet of the First Fire tells of the People following the sacred path and coming to reside on Turtle Island, a name many tribes use to refer to North America. During the Second Fire, the prophecy tells of the People moving to a large lake, but they begin to stray from the path of goodness and are brought back to it by a young boy. There is a western movement of the People during the Third Fire, and with the coming of the Fourth Fire it is told that the White man will appear.

In Steven McFadden's *Profiles in Wisdom,* Grandfather Commanda says:

> The fourth prophet told of the Fourth Fire, a time when light-skinned people would come to Turtle Island. If they came wearing the face of brotherhood, then there would come a time of wonderful change for generations. They would bring with them new knowledge, and new articles to join with the knowledge of this country. In this way the knowledge could all be joined together to make one mighty nation, and that nation would be joined by two more, so that the four nations would form the mightiest nation of all. We would know this if the light-skinned race came carrying no weapons—if they came bearing only their knowledge and a handshake. But another prophet said, "Beware if the light-skinned race comes wearing the face of death. You must be careful because the face of death and the face of brotherhood look very much alike. If they come carrying a weapon, beware. If they come in suffering, they could fool you. Their hearts may be filled with greed for the riches of this land. If they are indeed your brothers, let them prove it. Do not accept them in total trust. You shall know that the face they wear is the one of death if the rivers run with poison, and fish become unfit to eat. You shall know them by these things."

Grandson, you are well aware of the number of dead lakes, rivers, and poisoned fish. So many lakes and rivers even have warnings posted, telling people not to eat the fish they catch. So, unfortunately, as in many of the prophecies concerning the coming of the White man, the destruction warned of has come to pass. In the Fifth Fire, the prophet told of great struggles for the native peoples. It will, however, be a time when a message of salvation and extreme happiness is brought to the People.

But if they listen to this message and leave the teachings of the elders, then the Fifth Fire with its turmoil and disintegration shall continue for generations. The prophet warns that the "new promises" given to the People during this time by the light-skinned race will be deceitful and shall not come about. Those who take these promises to heart will add to the destruction of the People. Grandfather Commanda says that his people believe that the promise is that of the materialistic way of life of the Western Europeans, and the prophesied turmoil represents the wars against the Red man.

Grandfather Commanda continues:

> When the Sixth Fire came to be, the words of the prophet rang true, as children were taken away from the teachings of the elders. The boarding school era of "civilizing" Indian children had begun. The Indian language and religion were taken from the children. The people started dying at an early age. They had lost their will to live and their purpose in living.

Fortunately, there were wise men among the People who saw the possible loss of all their traditions. The very foundations of the Anishinabe spiritual life were at stake. Hopefully, to ensure their future, the priests of the Midewiwin Way decided that all of the sacred bundles and scrolls should be buried. They were placed in a hollowed-out ironwood tree and buried in the side of a cliff. The ceremonies remained only in the minds and hearts of the people. The old ones say that when it again becomes safe for the Anishinabe People to follow their ways without fear of the White man, "a little boy would dream where the Ironwood Log, full of sacred bundles and scrolls, was buried. He would lead his people to the place." Grandfather Commanda believes that the time will be soon.

The prophet of the Seventh Fire told of the emergence of a "new people." These people will be keenly aware that all is not right and will go back to the ancient ways of their People, retracing their steps. This backtracking will ultimately lead them to the elders, but unfortunately many of them will be in the state of torpor that His Crazy Horse foresaw. The journey of these "new people" will be a difficult one with so many of the elders asleep, others afraid to speak, and still others not even asked for their wisdom.

But the seventh prophet speaks with hope, for if the "new people" are persistent and courageous in their journey, then "the water drum of the Midewiwin Lodge [the sacred way] will again sound its voice." Should this occur, there will be a renewal, and the Anishinabe Nation shall rise again.

This renewal will signal a pivotal time in history. The Euro-American people will be faced with a choice of one of two paths. One is the continuation of the scientific, technological, and industrial path that has so damaged the Earth and her peoples. The other is the path of spirituality, which respects and nourishes the Earth. One choice will cause the destruction that they have brought to the world to rebound upon them and cause a purification. But if the other way is chosen, "then the Seventh Fire will light an eighth and final fire, an eternal fire of peace, love, brotherhood, and sisterhood."

According to Grandfather Commanda, we are quickly approaching this fork in the road. There must be a coming together of all the peoples of the world such that there is only "one mind," for "the Creator will not answer until you have just one mind, just like if you have one person."

The theme of "One Mind" is one that runs through many Indian cultures. Decisions were often put off if agreement could not be reached, for the very lack of agreement itself showed that the problem was a thorny one that dictated caution and reflection.

We are not a hurried people as you are. The Iroquois Nations were wise in looking unto the seventh generation before making a decision. One has only to look at the sorry state of the environment to appreciate the wisdom of the Iroquois. More often than not, the White culture wants decisions now, this minute, without thought or concern for the generations that will follow. This is both self-centered and short-sighted.

The children of today are living with the destructiveness of technological expertise untempered by wisdom. I'm sorry to say, Grandson, that the headlong rush for progress and profit has been at the expense of the physical, emotional, and spiritual health of your children. But you know this, and it is why you are here.

Thank you, Grandfather. The theme of polarities is really with us today, isn't it? And the question of choice. Grandfather Commanda's prophecies from the wampum belts are both frightening and hopeful. But I really think that more and more of us are facing the extremity of our situation and having some kind of spiritual awakening. But waking up is hard, Grandfather. As you often say, it's easier to ignore the pain of the present and grab whatever temporary pleasure you can.

Did you study philosophy in college, Grandson? The old philosopher Spinoza ended his major work, *Ethics,* by saying that all things beautiful are as difficult as they are rare. He was both right and wrong. In a society that does not particularly value the beautiful, the noble, the generous, and the life-giving, it is difficult. But when you live in a society in which you are surrounded by such things, it becomes a matter of course. It is hard to create a masterpiece from a garbage heap, but if one lives in and raises one's children in a masterpiece, then it is unthinkable to produce garbage. Among my People we called this honor, balance, and right relationship.

I suppose that Spinoza, like all philosophers, was coming from his own cultural perspective. I know I'm bound so much by the same worldview. I'm also bound by my love of creature comforts. Tell me, does Grandfather Commanda think that we have to get rid of all our technology? It's often said that technology isn't the problem; it's how we use it.

I truthfully do not know if he thinks that we need to abandon technology. But I do know that he believes that if we do not put the Earth and spirituality first, then we are headed for a very troubled time. The problem is that people seldom know where technology is leading. Just look at television. It has supplanted conversation in families. It has interfered with the transmission of experience, knowledge, and traditions between the generations. Children do not spend as much time playing, and their parents spend less time playing with them. This has lead to a stultification of imagination, which is so important for a healthy and creative mind. This does not even speak to the point that the brilliant educator, Joseph Chilton Pierce, makes: "The major damage of television has little to do with content: Its damage is neurological, and it has, indeed, damaged us, perhaps beyond repair."

This is just one problem with technology that we might discuss. I will tell you another because it almost happened to my grandson, Tommy's father. In 1948, he was having trouble with his sinuses. My son took him to the Indian Health Services, as the problem had become chronic. After the visit, he came to me to discuss what they wanted to do. They wanted to stick two prongs of radium up his nose and irradiate his sinuses. This was not an uncommon treatment at the time. It was, as they say, state of the art.

Fortunately, my son was wise enough not to let them perform the procedure. Years later it was found out that many people who had been irradiated in that way developed thyroid cancer. And if the air was not so polluted, I doubt he would have had the sinus problem in the first place. But one of our medicine carriers was able to cure him. So, Grandson, I do not know whether technology is good or bad. But like all knowledge, it is useless unless tempered by the true wisdom of interrelationship.

Grandfather, the Anishinabe prophecies spoke of Purifications if we went down the wrong road. Are there more prophecies like that?

There are many prophecies of purifications, or what are often called "Earth cleansings." They come from tribes as distant geographically as the Iroquois Nations of the New York area and the Hopi of the Southwest. These prophecies of the Purification of the Earth all seem, to me at least, to have the same theme. Unless the people of the world return to spiritual values, or the Original Instructions, and begin to clean up the mess they have made on Earth, both environmentally and socially, then Grandmother Earth will cleanse Herself.

For some it will be the work of the Earth itself, and for others the work of the Great Spirit, as the White man calls our Mysterious One. For others they will be acting in concert. It really does not matter. The point is that if the world and society are not brought back into balance, then there shall be a purging. For many tribes, the hurricanes, the tornadoes, the floods, and the earthquakes are all signs of the beginning of the purging.

According to some Haudenosaunee, the event that initiates this cleansing is supposed to occur when mankind begins to search for the "secrets of the Sun." This is taken to be nuclear energy by many Indian peoples, and it tells them that the Purification is at hand. For others among the Haudenosaunee, the time of the cleansing will be announced by the dying of the sacred elm trees from the top on down. This is happening now, Grandson, because of acid rain. The dying of the elms in their prophecies is to be followed by the dying of the maples. And so now this has also begun. The Haudenosaunee prophets also told of a time when it would be hard to tell men from women. And, at least to these old eyes, this has also come to pass among many of your young people.

Near the beginning of the Purification, the prophets told of the fish dying in the lakes and floating belly up. The final warning, they say, shall be when the strawberry bushes no longer yield their berries, but when only a red leaf shall appear on the bush.

All these warning signs have come to pass except for the demise of the strawberry, and when that occurs, the cleansing shall begin in earnest. According to several tribes, this will be the fourth time that the Earth has had to be cleansed because of human greed and imbalance.

Don't the Hopi have fairly complex and involved prophecies about this Purification or cleansing? I heard somewhere that they have already had the closing ceremonies for this world. From what little I know, their prophecies seem to be the most well known. Will you tell me about them?

The Hopi do have very old and specific prophecies, which, so far, have come to pass. However, I can say little about them out of respect for the Hopi. I know that many volumes have been written about these prophecies, and that some elders from the Hopi Nation have tried to communicate them to people in power and even to the United Nations. But this has caused conflict, and, at times, bad feelings among them. For instance, when the good friend of the Indian, Frank Waters, published his *Book of the Hopi* in 1963, many of the elders and Kiva priests were mighty upset. Some writers on the Hopi prophecies have even been banned from the reservation.

Many White people think that just because someone is an elder and a full-blood, they have the knowledge and authority to speak about the tribe and its prophecies. This is not so, and some of the prophecies that have made their way into print are incorrect. Others should not be spoken of out of respect for the wishes of the Hopi. Even at my age, there are many things I would not speak about concerning our people without consulting the appropriate elders, medicine carriers, or, perhaps, even the Keeper of the Sacred Pipe or the Sacred Arrows, if necessary. There is much, how do you say it?—phony stuff—being brought out these days concerning the Indian Peoples. This misinformation, and at times correct information that should not be released, has come not only from White people but from what Lakota elder Matthew King calls "plastic medicine men." Beware of them.

On October 5, 1980, at the fifth annual meeting of the Traditional Elders Circle, a resolution was passed. It states in part:

> It has been brought to the attention of the Elders and their representatives in Council that various individuals are moving about this Great Turtle Island and across the great waters to foreign soil, purporting to be spiritual leaders. They carry pipes and other objects sacred to Red Nations, the indigenous people of the western hemisphere. These individuals are gathering non-Indian people as followers who believe they are receiving instructions of the original people. We the Elders and our representatives sitting in Council give warning to these non-Indian followers that it is our understanding this is not a proper process and the authority to carry these sacred objects is given by the people and the purpose and procedure are specific to the time and the needs of the people. . . . Therefore, be warned that these individuals are moving about playing upon the needs and ignorance of our non-Indian brothers and sisters. The value of these instructions and ceremonies is questionable, maybe meaningless, and hurtful to the individual carrying false messages.

The Elders even asked that people write to them, and they will do their best to find out the truth of the matter in question. The real medicine carriers that I know are all quite poor and dedicated to the People. They are not flying around giving workshops and charging money to attend sweat lodges. This does not mean that occasionally real medicine people do not talk in public or do ceremonies with non-Indians present. They do. It also does not mean they do not accept donations to help meet their needs. But they do not advertise or solicit funds. As the Onondaga elder Louis Farmer said, "You want to know who's a real medicine man? He's the one who doesn't say 'I'm a medicine man.' He doesn't ask you to come to him. You've got to go and ask him. And you'll find he's always there among his own people."

The Council of Elders concluded:

> We concern ourselves only with those people who use spiritual ceremonies with non-Indian people for profit. There are many things to be shared with the Four Colors of humanity in our common destiny as one with our Mother the Earth. It is this sharing that must be considered with great care by the Elders and the medicine people who carry the Sacred Trusts, so that no harm may come to people through ignorance and misuse of these powerful forces.

But, returning to the Hopi, Grandson, yes, if we do not change our ways, they believe that there will be a Great Purification and that most of the signs are in place. The choice is up to us.

I'm sorry, Grandfather, if I asked something I shouldn't have.

There is nothing to be sorry about, Grandson. You asked a question in good faith, and I answered in the same spirit. You see, Indian religion or spirituality is not something that can be, or is, taught like many other religions. There are no catechism classes or Sunday schools. Furthermore, Indian spirituality involves the community and a dedication to that community and the joyful willingness to sacrifice for the good of the People.

We are not in the business of making disaffected people feel good. We are in the business of preserving our People and our traditions, and of serving each other. One cannot simply say I am an Indian like one can say I am a Catholic or a Hindu. If you are not putting the People first, then you are no Indian, regardless of the color of your skin. Every Indian must, in some sense, be a warrior. It may not be on the battlefield as in the old days, although at times that may also occur as at Wounded Knee Two in 1973. It may be in the courts, at an alcohol treatment center, or wherever the People need help and support.

I'm beginning to understand that it's impossible to separate true Indian spiritual beliefs from actions in daily life. That's a principle we also value in my culture. We say that a person's actions speak louder than their words.

That is exactly what worried His Crazy Horse about the United States government. They said one thing and did another, which was impossible for him to understand in the context of his own culture. Their promises meant nothing. But it is not too late to keep some of those promises when people of good heart, like you, understand the true story of American history. And if enough people choose the right road, together we might create a new world and learn from the mistakes of the past. Otherwise, perhaps a Purification is inevitable.

Some of the other prophecies of purification that I can tell you about are those of the Zuni, for they have published them in a book called *Zunis: Self Portrayals*. These prophecies deal with both things that have occurred and things that are likely to happen in the future if people and nations do not change their ways. Let me read to you, Grandson:

Many years ago when our grandparents foresaw what our future would be like, they spoke about their prophecies among themselves and passed them on to the children before them: "Cities will progress and then decay to the ways of the lowest beings. Drinkers of dark liquids will come upon the land, speaking nonsense and filth. Then the end shall be near. Population will increase until the land can hold no more. The tribes of men will mix. The dark liquids they drink will cause the people to fight among themselves. Families will break up: father against children and the children against one another. Maybe when the people have outdone themselves, then maybe, the stars will fall upon the land, or drops of hot water will rain upon the Earth. Or the land will turn under. Or our father, the sun, will not rise to start the day. Then our possessions will turn into beasts and devour us whole. If not, there will be an odor from gases, which will fill the air we breathe, and the end for us shall come. But the people themselves will bring upon themselves what they receive. From what has resulted, time alone will tell what the future holds for us."

It hurts to hear these things, Grandfather. Our cities have certainly gone through periods of prosperity, but so many are now laying in decay. In many ways our cities are wastelands of pollution, social disruption, and physical and structural decline. The streets are unsafe, crime is rampant, and there is so much anonymity and disconnectedness among the people who live there. I guess that the dark liquids the Zuni spoke of are various kinds of alcoholic drinks. Addiction is almost a national pastime, after all, and alcohol certainly brings out the worst violent tendencies in a lot of people.

And, as the Zuni say, a lot of intergenerational respect has been lost, and parents can hardly control their kids anymore. The mention of children turning against one another is especially disturbing. The gang wars, shootings, beatings, and stabbings of kids in the streets are all so saddening. We're already at the point where the air is filled with noxious gases. Do you think that the Zunis see the end of the world approaching very soon?

I am not sure. But, once again, Grandson, pay attention to the element of choice. Whether the prophecy refers only to the Zuni or to the world as a whole, which I think it does, we are running out of time to make constructive choices. Just look at Africa. Many nations there have more than 50 percent of their population testing positive for the HIV virus. And, we do know that many of the new and threatening diseases that are beginning to arise have been brought about by our destruction of the natural world.

I cannot say what will happen, Grandson, for I am not a prophet, but I can tell you this with certainty: Humankind must act, and act soon, to stem the tide of destructiveness that is causing the Earth to become uninhabitable. I do not believe that the solution will come from technology, and unfortunately that is what most people are counting on. Only a spiritual revolution will save us.

I read a book last year by Leakey and Lewin, who are well-known paleobiologists. It was shocking to find out that 80 living species a day are becoming extinct. This disappearance of life is occurring at 120,000 times the normal rate of extinction, and is unparalleled in what they call "normal" times. That is, times other than the five major periods of extinction when some major natural force shifted the Earth's balance, like when the dinosaurs disappeared.

Perhaps you would consider Leakey and Lewin scientific prophets, Grandfather, because they believe this rapid rate of anthropogenic—or human-caused—extinction will soon make the Earth uninhabitable. They predict that either human beings will become extinct or that our social and economic structures will disintegrate as the Earth quickly becomes more and more unbalanced.

Once again, Grandson, your scientists corroborate what indigenous peoples have always known. All natural systems are interdependent, and harm in any one sector inevitably causes problems in other places that only show up over a period of time.

And by the time the damage becomes obvious, it may be impossible to restore any semblance of balance.

Let me end our conversation by telling you the story of White Buffalo Calf Woman, who came to the Lakota with a message of hope and renewal. Long, long ago, there came a time when food was scarce. The chiefs sent two young men out to search for buffalo, that the people might be fed. They were not having any luck, so they climbed a hill from where they could see far over the great plains. In the distance, they noticed that something was walking toward them. As the figure got closer, they knew that it must be a sacred being of some sort, for it floated more than it walked.

As the figure came closer, the two young men could see that it was a young woman. In front of her, she carried both a bundle and a fan of sage. She was a beautiful and radiant young woman, dressed in colors so magnificent and clear that they could not have been of this Earth. Her exquisite dress had sacred markings and quillwork such as the boys had never seen before. The young woman who approached them was White Buffalo Calf Woman— a holy woman of great power.

She was more beautiful than any woman that either of the young men had ever seen or imagined. Unfortunately, one of the boys began to have less than pure thoughts about the maiden, and as he approached her, he was struck down by lightning. All that remained was a pile of burned bones. White Buffalo Calf Woman called the other young man to her side and instructed him to go back to his village and report everything he had seen. He was also to tell the People that she was from the Buffalo Nation and had messages for them. He did what he was told and informed the chief of all that had passed.

The chief listened to the young man with great respect and told the entire village to prepare for the arrival of a spirit being. The largest and most sacred of the medicine tipis was raised and prepared. The People waited, and after four days, they saw the holy woman approaching the village carrying a large bundle. When she arrived, the chief escorted her to the medicine lodge, which she entered and circled in the direction of the sun.

Next, she prepared an altar with a buffalo skull and taught the People a number of sacred rituals and how to perform them in a good way. When that was done, she took from her bundle the Sacred Pipe, the *chanupa wakan*, one of the greatest spiritual gifts that our People has ever received. She taught us that the smoke that arose from the pipe was the sacred breath of The Great Mysterious, which would carry our prayers to the Sacred Ones.

"With this holy pipe," she said, "you will walk like a living prayer. With your feet resting upon the Earth and the pipestem reaching into the sky, your body forms a living bridge between the Sacred Beneath and the Sacred Above. The *Wakan Tanka* [Great Spirit] smiles upon us, because we are now as one: Earth, sky, all living things, the two-legged, the four-legged, the winged ones, the trees, the grasses. Together with the People they are all related, one family."

White Buffalo Calf Woman talked with the women of the village that they might remember their great importance and role in the life of the tribe, for it was the women who sustained the tribe. She also talked to the children, reminding them that they were the future of the tribe and must prepare themselves in a good and sacred way. She addressed the tribe as a whole, saying that they were a pure and good people and that for that reason, the Sacred Pipe was entrusted to them. However, this trust was not for them alone, but for all the People.

White Buffalo Calf Woman took leave of the Lakota, promising that she would return in the future should there be times of great need. As she walked away toward the West, she rolled over four times. After the first roll, she turned into a black buffalo; after the second roll, a brown buffalo; after the third roll, a red buffalo; and, finally, after the fourth roll, she turned into a white buffalo calf. At this point White Buffalo Calf Woman walked into the horizon and could be seen no more.

From that time on, the Buffalo Nation came in great herds to supply the People with all they needed for food, clothing, and shelter. And the white buffalo became the most sacred of all of Earth's creatures for the Lakota. In the third week of August in 1994, a white buffalo calf was born on a small farm in Wisconsin. For the Lakota, and many other Indian Nations, this was an occasion for great rejoicing and hope, for it meant that the prayers of the People were still being heard and that the old ways of the Indians were returning.

As you know now, Grandson, traditional Indian life is in great jeopardy as the dominant culture continues oppressing Indian religion and culture, making it more and more difficult to live as the Creator would like us to. The birth of the white buffalo gives us hope, and yet at the same time, a warning. The warning is simple: If the People are to continue, they must retain the old ways or they shall be lost in the mists of time. More and more Indians are returning to the ways of their ancestors, but if this resurgence does not continue, then when White Buffalo Calf Woman appears again, all will be lost for the Red man.

Already the calf born in Wisconsin has changed color three times, from white to black, to brown, to red. The People await her turning white again, a sign that the prayers of the Lakota are still being heard and answered. According to many elders, there will be four white buffaloes born, and to date, three have appeared, along with three partially white ones. This is also notice to the People that their prayers are being heard.

Of course, our medicine people are all free to interpret the coming of the white buffalo calf as their visions dictate. Our religion is not static, but fluid and responsive to the demands and the situations in which the People find themselves. For some elders, the birth of the white buffalo calf and the four colors represent the four races of humankind and the resurgence of the feminine power. This will lead to a new day for all, but perhaps not before there is some kind of purification through either natural or man-made disasters, and those in power are replaced.

Arvol Looking Horse is the Keeper of the Pipe given to us by White Buffalo Calf Woman. His family has been the Keeper of the Sacred Pipe for 19 generations, and he was only 12 years old when the responsibility was passed to him by his grandmother. According to him:

> Now we are in a critical stage of our spiritual, moral and technological development as nations. All life is precariously balanced. We must remember that all things on Mother Earth have a spirit and are intricately related. The mending of the sacred hoop of all nations, prophesied by the Lakota, has begun. May we find in the ancient wisdom of the indigenous nations, the spirit and courage to mend and heal.

There were elders, such as Floyd Hand, who dreamed of the white buffalo calf being born when she was. When the calf was born, he drove from the Pine Ridge Reservation to Wisconsin to see her at the farm of Dave and Val Heider. In his vision of the birth of the calf, Hand had seen that the father of the white buffalo "would lay down his life for the calf." According to his vision, there was some kind of mass deep in the bull's intestines that would cause its death. This is exactly what happened, Grandson. Just 12 days after the birth of the white calf, the father died and the autopsy revealed an obstruction in his intestines. Such is the power of our medicine carriers' dreams and visions.

White Buffalo Calf Woman reminds me a little bit of some stories I've heard about the Jewish prophet Elijah. He is also a spirit being, having left the Earth in a fiery chariot. He returns in difficult times to give guidance, and may come in any kind of disguise. I often think of him when I pass street beggars. Any person could be a spirit being, or an angel, I suppose. But I still feel sorry for the young man who was lusting over the beautiful White Buffalo Calf Woman and then got turned into a bone pile when he was struck by lightning.

Lusting after things that are not ours often has such results, Grandson, even if they are not so immediate and dramatic. Think of the expressions—consumed with jealousy, or burning up with lust or anger. Then think of the bad actions that these unchecked emotions can create. Spirit Beings can take ordinary chains of cause and effect and present them in a condensed way that makes the point very clearly.

I see what you mean, Grandfather. There's often such a lag between what we do and the results that happen that we miss the connection.

That is why the warrior stays aware of his or her motivations, Grandson. Now let me end our session with a prophecy known by few non-Indians. According to several tribes in the United States such as the Hopi and the Pit River Nation, and to indigenous peoples in places as far away as Africa, India, and Vietnam, there exists a spirit who lives upon the Earth and watches over it. This spirit is the caretaker of the Earth and the most powerful being upon it, although not as powerful as the Above Beings. Rather, this spirit is a kind of intermediary between Earth and more powerful beings not of this Earth.

It is told in the prophecies of these peoples that this spirit will return and make itself known. Throughout history, this spirit being has communicated with humans through dreams and visions. The Hopi call this Earth Spirit, Massau. Massau's reappearance will tell us that we are at a crossroads in human history. Either we correct our ways or there will be a Great Purification caused by forsaking our responsibilities to the Earth.

According to Craig Carpenter, a Mohawk who has spent much of his life as an intertribal messenger, learning from the elders and medicine carriers of many indigenous peoples, this great Earth Spirit began to appear again in October of 1958. To many he is known as Bigfoot. Yet Bigfoot's return has a message of hope, for he prophesied that he would come back so that justice might be returned to the human nations. So, you see, Grandson, many of the indigenous nations of both the Americas and other parts of the world are giving us fair warning. The question is, will we listen, or will our greed lead to even more disastrous consequences than we are already experiencing?

So do you think we will be able to come back to balance soon enough, Grandfather, or will there be an Earth cleansing?

I have little doubt that there will be purification of some sort, Grandson. In fact, it has already started. One sign is the new diseases that are emerging, everything from AIDS and chronic fatigue syndrome to ebola. And your scientists tell us that there will be more sicknesses, as viruses that have lived for millennia in the ancient forests are released when massive areas are slashed and burned to create more space to grow crops for a few years. Other signs are the breakdown of the social web in the Western nations: the increases in crime, racial and class struggles, alienation, the suffering of the children, addiction, depression, loss of intergenerational contact, and mistaking material improvement for progress. As fear and insecurity escalate, governments try harder to exert control over every aspect of life, and there is also a rise in dogmatic and fundamentalist religions that prey upon fear and the helplessness that pervades so many people's lives.

On the positive side, more and more people are becoming spiritual seekers, and there is a resurgence of the feminine and the intrinsic female understanding of right relationship and interrelatedness. The women, as any Indian nation knows, are the real receptacles of power. But there is a problem here. If women choose to abrogate this gift and become as men, then I see little hope. It is the women of the world who must stand up and say, "Enough is enough! We will no longer support your destruction, your war, and your violence toward life. We will no longer give our sons as pawns in your games of power and destruction, which benefit the few and harm the many while your lies make them believe that they are being served. We are the daughters of Earth, and we will be heard!"

The work of the environmental groups such as Greenpeace is also very positive. They make it harder and harder for people to deny the reality of the situation that we now face. Also, by standing up for the Earth, they unite the peoples of the world in a common cause that knows no political or national boundaries. They can truly act as brothers in protecting our common Mother.

So, if I understand what you've been saying, you see us in a titanic struggle for survival and wholeness on the one hand, and destructiveness and illness on the other. We're back to the polarity where we started. Is that fair?

I would say so. We are at a crossroads. It is up to the human family to choose life, in the fullest sense, or continual death and destruction. We have reached the time of the great Either/Or, and those who sit on the fence shall be as responsible as those who choose death. Either the enormity of the situation is faced, or there may be nothing to face at all.

Tomorrow I will begin to tell you how we, as a People, used to live, and maybe from that you can begin to create blueprints for a future that is really worth living. It is time for the dominant culture to become the students, and for the indigenous peoples of Earth to be their teachers. It may be your only salvation.

I will end by teaching you a song that His Crazy Horse received from The Great Mysterious. Then we will go sweat and purify our bodies, minds, and spirits that we, too, may hear The Great Mysterious and take heart.

My friend,
They will return again.
All over the Earth,
They are returning again.
Ancient teachings of the Earth,
Ancient songs of the Earth,
They are returning again.
My friend, they are returning.
I give them to you,
And through them
You will understand,
You will see.
They are returning again
Upon the Earth.

Ⓧ   Ⓧ   Ⓧ

CHAPTER SIX

SPIRITUALITY AND A NEW INTEGRAL CULTURE

The red fox was a trickster. Grooming her long whiskers with block-stockinged legs, she sent a sly glance to John and then ran off into the darkness of the predawn woods. Over the last few days, she had formed the habit of waiting for him and leading him to unexpected places. Twitching her long, bushy tail, she took off to the East and ran just slow enough for John to keep pace. The dawn was impatient to give birth to the sun, and John wondered whether he should return to the cabin to greet the new day with Chasing Deer or continue to follow the fox. But when he tried to turn around, she backtracked and appeared on the trail ahead of him.

"Okay, little sister. I get the message. Lead on." The trail they followed was not for two-leggeds, but for four-leggeds. Elk spoor appeared like little clumps of shiny marbles, and fresh hoofprints marked the narrow way. In a mile or so, the trail opened out onto a small pond, glowing with the first rosy light of dawn. There stood a mother elk and her young one, silhouetted in the rays of Grandfather Sun. On the opposite bank was a brown bear standing on its hind legs, bigger than any animal John had ever seen.

Apparently unperturbed by the two-legged visitor, it dropped to all fours and drank, the smooth water sending out ripples all around it.

The fox dipped her dainty paw into the water, also sending out ripples. Soon they intersected with those of the bear, and new patterns of energy moved across the shimmering water. The fox actually seemed to nod at John, and he slowly moved forward, several yards from the elk. Like the bear, he dropped down on all fours and scooped up some of the clear water to drink. His ripples also moved across the still pond, and as he drank the sweet waters, he felt the deep warmth of solidarity with the Earth and all her creatures.

John: Good morning, Grandfather. I know I'm late. Hope you weren't worried about me.

Chasing Deer: I saw two sets of tracks going East, Grandson—yours and the fox's. You cannot fool an old Indian. And the fox cannot fool me either. She knows that words are but pale shadows of the spirit world, and she wanted you to experience our lesson in your body, in your heart. What did she teach you of spirituality, John?

In just a week here, my relationship to nature has deepened so much, Grandfather, although the natural world has always been a sanctuary for me. The fox showed me how we are all related. If the bear drinks, it touches me. And if I drink, it touches the bear and the fox and the elk. All our ripples are present in the waters of life, and everything is connected.

Sister Fox is a good teacher. You have asked me to explain the spiritual and religious life of the Indian, and she has given you the first lesson. Everything is connected and filled with meaning. For us, the natural world is alive, intelligent, and infused with both Spirit and spirits. Indian scholar and lawyer Vine Deloria writes in *God is Red*:

> There are . . . many other entities with spiritual powers comparable to those generally attributed to one deity above. So many in fact that they must simply be encountered and appeased; they cannot be counted. In addition, all inanimate entities have spirit and personality so that the mountains, rivers, waterfalls—even the continent and the Earth itself— have intelligence, knowledge, and the ability to communicate ideas. The physical world is so filled with life and personality that humans appear as one minor species without much signif- icance and badly in need of assistance from other life forms. Almost anyone can have almost any relationship with anything else. So much energetic potency exists that we either must describe everything as religious or say that religion as we have known it is irrelevant to our concerns.

So you can see, nature is our temple, our cathedral. The fox and the bear, the rocks and trees are our teachers and priests. Our ances- tral lands were as loved as our own Grandfathers, and we treated them with the same respect. Our history, our religion, cannot be sep- arated from the land. There is for each tribe a sacred geography, and to destroy this is to destroy the People. Around 1900, when the gov- ernment wanted to take her People's land, Cecilio Blacktooth spoke eloquently for all her Indian Brothers and Sisters:

> You ask us to think what place we like next best to this, where we have always lived. You see the graveyard there? These are our fathers and grandfathers. You see that Eagle-nest mountain and that Rabbit-hole mountain? When God made them, He gave us this place. We have always been here. . . . This is our home. . . . We cannot live anywhere else. . . . If you will

not buy this place, we will go into the mountains like quail, and die there, the old people, and the women and children. . . .

When Andrew Jackson had the Choctaw removed from their ancestral home to Oklahoma, ". . . the women made a formal procession through the trees surrounding their abandoned cabins, stroking the leaves of the oak and elm trees in silent farewell." And when the land of Chief Seath'tl's people was taken, he said:

> Every part of all this soil is sacred to my people. Every hill-side, every valley, every plain and grove has been hallowed by some sad or happy event in days long vanished. The very dust you now stand on responds more willingly to their footsteps than to yours, because it is rich with the blood of our ancestors, and our bare feet are conscious of the sympathetic touch.

When representatives of the Lakota and the Haudenosaunee went to a global human rights conference in Geneva, Switzerland, as representatives of the native peoples of the Americas, Chief Oren Lyons said of the conference:

> There is a hue and a cry for human rights . . . "for the peoples." And the indigenous people said, "What of the rights of the natural world? Where is the seat for the Buffalo or the Eagle? Who is representing them here in your forum? Who is speaking for the waters of the Earth? Who is speaking for the trees and the forest? Who is speaking for the Fish, for the Whales, for the Beavers, for our children?"

I hope that my generation will speak for the children, Grandfather, as so many others of conscience are already doing. I've been so impressed with the work of Marion Wright Edelman of the Children's Defense Fund. She speaks out with a strong, compassionate voice. She wrote a stirring public letter to President Clinton challenging him to put federal money where his mouth is, remarking that it would be a shame if the children were ignored on his watch since he speaks so passionately for them. And as for the trees and animals, there are more and more people like the Greenpeace activists who are beginning to realize that the natural world can't simply be exploited as a resource. That it is alive, intelligent, and that the destruction of species has a profound effect on the life of humans that can't be measured through simple economics. I know that there's a long way to go, Grandfather, but I see more people committed to saving the Earth and her children—not just the human children, but all the children, all the creatures. Perhaps there is still time to turn the situation around and avert the Purification. Everything I've learned from you tells me that Grandmother Earth will not let her children continue to suffer, and if she has to create a time of chaos to turn the situation around, she will.

I know that when you are a lawyer, Grandson, you will also fight for the land and all the children who live upon it—whether it is protection of Park Service land from logging or protection of Native lands. Much of our homeland is gone now, but the rest is a place of power that benefits not only the People on the reservations, but all human beings of the world. This land where we sit is sacred to generations of Indians and to me personally. I can show you where my father was born, where my mother was born, where the spirits of the stones first talked to me, where I first kissed my wife, where my *kola* (the deepest of friends for whom one would willingly sacrifice his life), Swift Elk, and I sealed our lifelong commitment to each other. I can show you where Tommy took his first steps, where I had my first sweat lodge, and where all the moments that make up a lifetime were lived. Every part of me is tied to our Lakota land. Here the fox and the eagle know me and send me their greetings and wisdom when I need it. Here I lie upon the ground, and the pulsing vibrations of Grandmother heal my weariness. I am the land, and the land is me.

It seems that my culture, and at least the Christianity I was raised with, have lost touch with the natural world. And in separating Earth and heaven, we've devalued the Earth. I read recently that one-third of the agricultural land on the planet has already been covered by buildings and roads. So now the rain forests are being cut down to provide more agricultural land, which is fertile for only three to five years before it turns to dust. I worry that, soon, perhaps even in the generation of my own grandchildren, there won't be enough trees and vegetation remaining to provide oxygen to breathe. And when the old-growth forests are cut down, the watersheds are also destroyed. Without air and water, Grandfather, there is no more life—or at least life as we have known it—and we will have brought the Purification upon ourselves. The trouble is that many people know this, but we don't know how to stop it.

The very interconnectedness that you define as indigenous spirituality is part of the problem in finding a solution that will stop the destruction of the Earth. Every time a change occurs in one sector, it affects something else. When loggers in the Pacific Northwest think that their jobs will end because of protecting the habitat of the Spotted Owl, there is such pain. How will they feed their children? Sparing the trees seems to mean harming their families. But the Spotted Owl isn't the real issue—it's just a symptom of the massive extinction that cutting down the old forests represents. And in a few years there won't be many old trees left, and the loggers will have to find other jobs. A huge amount of the old timber doesn't go to American sawmills to provide jobs, anyway. It's exported to Japan, which is willing to pay more for the logs because they won't cut their own forests and damage the water supply. The entire global economy, which is intricately interconnected, makes the problem hard to solve, Grandfather.

As an Indian, I do not find it easy to understand these things, Grandson, whether it is the separation of Earth and heaven or of anything from its relations. For example, how can pesticides be used to kill insects without realizing that they will eventually kill all animals, including the two-leggeds? Or take the problem of crime. Those who do evil are caught and put in jail, yet there is little effort to heal them there and reconnect them with their own good hearts. Even less effort is given to addressing the social problems of children that shape them into criminals to begin with. To avoid the Purification and gather all nations under the Great Tree of Peace, I have said repeatedly that there must be a global spiritual awakening, especially in what you call First World countries that are the major consumers of natural resources. Fortunately, that spiritual awakening is beginning. Have you read the study of sociologist Paul Ray?

No, Grandfather. What did he find?

Ray has documented a new social movement among 44 million Americans, 24 percent of the population, whom he calls Cultural Creatives or CCs. This group began to emerge in the 1970s and has grown rapidly, drawing on feminine values. And as I have said, it is the women who are key to saving the planet and bringing back the values of interrelatedness. They understand that every person and every thing comes into its fullest expression of being through relationship, and that holiness and respectful relationship are one.

There are two groups of CCs: the Core Cultural Creatives and the Green Cultural Creatives. Core CCs number 20 million and are environmentally concerned, intent upon building community, interested in learning about the wisdom of cultures and religions other than their own, and concerned with psychological growth and spirituality. These are the cutting-edge thinkers and trend-setters, and there are twice as many women as men in this group. Green CCs number 23 million, or 13 percent of the population, and have values centered on ecological sustainability from a more secular point of view. They take their lead from the core CCs.

Ray writes about two other major groups in American society: Modernists and Traditionalists. The Traditionalists have their roots in medieval Europe and tend to be rural, racist, and fearful of cultures and religions other than their own. They value strong community, but unfortunately, exclusive kinds of community. They represent 29 percent of the population, or 56 million people. The Modernists, whose roots go back 500 years to the end of the Renaissance, have values centered on economics, military strength, technology, and intellectual growth. Both liberals and conservatives are found within Modernist culture. The newest group, Grandson, barely 30 years old, are the Cultural Creatives who, according to Ray, go beyond environmentalism to an appreciation of the land and all of nature as sacred. Their values, I believe, are close to my own and that of indigenous spirituality. And they are activists who care about real change rather than Band-Aids. When they talk about curbing violence, they do not mean increasing police presence and jail sentences, but caring for the children in a way that produces caring adults. They are rebuilding communities and trying to alter the material world through spiritual values. So I am hopeful that this rapidly growing group of people with good heart can bring about the beautiful vision of His Crazy Horse.

Well, at least I have something to identify with now, Grandfather. I'm a Cultural Creative. But does Ray think that this group will have to overtake Traditionalists and Modernists for a new culture to be born?

No, Grandson, that is the beauty of his thinking. He believes that all groups have something good to offer in spite of their shortcomings, and that under the leadership of Cultural Creatives the best can be brought together in a new Integral Culture that preserves and honors diversity. When His Crazy Horse saw people of all colors and beliefs together under the Great Tree of

Peace, he was surprised and somewhat confounded. How could those whom he considered oppressors be among the seeds of a new era? And yet, Grandson, that is exactly what is happening. It has been difficult for me to envision such a future myself. And at times I grow melancholy longing for the past, for the old days and the old ways before the Europeans came to this land. I honor those traditional Indians who keep the old wisdom alive, for we must learn from them as His Crazy Horse foresaw. But I also know that we cannot live in the past, for much of the land is gone now. It takes courage, forgiveness, and a bold heart to let go of the old and create a new future. That, Grandson, is our task. And we have so little time.

There's a lot of talk about the millennium, Grandfather. American Indian prophecy isn't the only place where purification is mentioned. From the Revelations of St. John to the prophecies of Nostradamus to the Fatima Prophecies of the Virgin Mary, a time of great upheaval is predicted. Do you think that the prophecies of the Great Tree of Peace and the Purification may both be correct? That the old system needs to be wiped out before a new era can begin? The Nobel Prize–winning physicist Ilya Prigogine discovered something called The Law of Dissipative Structures. It states that whether we're talking about solar systems, molecular events, or cultures, the old structure has to disintegrate into chaos for a new structure of a higher order to emerge.

You may be right, Grandson, in thinking that at least some level of purification will precede the dawning of a new era. But I believe that the extent of that purification is up to us. If we continue on the same path, Grandmother Earth will purify herself, and perhaps many of us will die in the process. Viruses such as HIV and Ebola that may have been released from the cutting down of the rain forests are just one case in point. Many of your best scientists see a time of great plagues ahead. In just 40 years, the population of Earth will double from five to ten billion souls. Grandmother will not be able to sustain so many. So perhaps plagues will be needed to bring the planet into balance. To avoid this sorrow and heartache, the cutting down of the rain forests must be stopped, and population growth curbed drastically.

A few years ago, I would have thought that such change was impossible. But I also thought that the Berlin Wall would never fall. A lot of my friends are Cultural Creatives, Grandfather, and I can see how rapidly the consciousness of this country is changing. Money used to be the benchmark of success, and for many people it still is, but a lot of my friends don't want to grow up like their parents, always stressed and exhausted from trying to make a buck. A lot of us are willing to make less money so that we can have more time for friends and family. And also so that we can consume less and live in better balance with the land.

I once read an article about the wealthiest people in the United States, and so many of them had miserable lives and finally committed suicide. My people, on the other hand, do not have enough money to live, and many are miserable on account of hunger. But spirituality is available to all, rich and poor, and when we restore right relationship between the Earth and all her creatures, everyone will have enough. The problems we have discussed are difficult ones, Grandson, but like the Berlin Wall, they can suddenly give way to solution. I do not mean to sound glib, for the solutions will not be easy. A course of treatment for a disease often changes an individual's life for the worse in the beginning, but it can lead not only to the continuation of life, but to a new appreciation and gratitude for a life that was previously taken for granted.

When you speak of spirituality that is available to all, and spirituality as a necessity to realize the vision of His Crazy Horse, I get a little uncomfortable. To some people, spirituality is no more than loving thoughts, Grandfather. Love may be a noble sentiment, but it has to translate into action. A friend of mine who graduated last year and went into the restaurant business took me to a spirituality-in-business meeting in his town. One of the members was a clothing manufacturer whose garments are made in sweatshops in Guatemala. His idea of spirituality was establishing what are called "quality circles" for his management team in the States and meditating every night. Don't get me wrong, Grandfather, because both of those actions are good ones. Still, how can his business be spiritual when it rests on the shoulders of the poor who are given too little for their labor?

Spirituality can come in steps, Grandson, each person growing according to his or her own nature. Perhaps this businessman, through listening to his managers, through going to those meetings, or through hearing the Voice of The Great Mysterious in meditation, will realize your point. There can be no true spirituality when profits are made on the backs of the poor, because the relationship is inequitable.

You're more patient than I am, Grandfather.

I am much older, too, Grandson. I have seen many people change. For some, the change takes a long time while personal ego and the sense of specialness give way to being part of a larger community. That was the case with the prophet Sweet Medicine, whose life was eventually given for the good of the people. For others, chaos-creating events may play a part in developing spiritual values. People get sick, they lose their money, a loved one dies. Life as usual no longer exists, and they are thrown into a period of darkness and confusion. These tragedies make them think, *What is life all about?* And in the end, spirituality blossoms as they realize that the only thing that brings happiness is loving relationship. But other people change in the twinkling of an eye like the slave trader who was hit with a bolt of Divine Grace during a stormy ocean passage. He repented his lack of understanding, changed his ways, and wrote that beautiful spiritual, "Amazing Grace."

I've always loved that song, Grandfather. When it says, "I once was lost but now I'm found, was blind but now I see," it always reminds me of those moments in my own life when I've been suddenly and irrevocably changed for the better by some mysterious force. I guess grace is as good a word as any for that kind of sudden awakening.

The Great Mysterious wants all the children of the Earth to be happy, to find their way again. So grace is always available because love is the substance of the Mystery. But when we intend the good, Grandson, when we pray to The Great Mysterious for help in healing ourselves, one another, or the planet, that grace flows most abundantly. While I agree wholeheartedly that prayer in and of itself is an incomplete spirituality without right action to accompany it, do not underestimate its power. If all people of good heart from every culture continue to pray for the Earth, then changes will come that none of us could have ever imagined.

There's a lot of interest in the power of prayer, Grandfather. I've even read about scientific studies conducted on sick people who were being prayed for. Even though they didn't know that prayers were being said for them, and their doctors didn't either, the prayed for patients healed faster than those who weren't prayed for. So there's something that creates change above and beyond our own attitudes and beliefs. This spiritual power is so amazing. But please, Grandfather, remember, I'm a Cultural Creative, and I love to hear about the beliefs of other cultures. Tell me more about American Indian spirituality so that I can expand my understanding and take more informed action.

The mythologist Joseph Campbell said of Indians that there was probably not a more spiritual people to be found anywhere on Earth. And the foremost anthropologist of this century, Claude Levi-Strauss, remarked after several years of living with the Bororos, that "few people are so profoundly religious . . . few possess a metaphysical system of such complexity. Their spiritual beliefs and everyday activities are inextricably mixed."

Now it seems to me that some Westerners tend to see people like us as primitive and the intertwining of our religion with all our other activities as atavistic, even childish. But those who have truly lived with us seem in full agreement with Levi-Strauss when he said, "A primitive people is not a backward or retarded people. Indeed, it may possess a genius for invention or action that leaves the achievements of civilized people far behind."

Now, Grandson, I should make one thing clear before we go any further. To the best of anyone's knowledge, there were somewhere between 550 and 600 different tribes in what we presently call North America before the coming of the Europeans. While it is true that many beliefs and ceremonies were shared, or at least had similarities among tribes in close proximity to one another, there were also great differences.

Even in tribes that shared the same language family such as the Haudenosaunee Confederation, or some of the Plains tribes that lived in close proximity like the seven bands of the Lakota, the Cheyenne, and the Arapaho, each group had their own stories, and in some cases, even their creation stories were different.

Despite these differences, there are at least two things that we can say without fear of contradiction or offense. First of all, most tribes held similar views of nature, and second, they shared ideas of appropriate human behavior within the natural world, not necessarily in specific detail, but certainly generically. It is also wise to remember, Grandson, that I am a Cheyenne/Lakota, and I lived most of my life with my father's people—that is, the Lakota. Seldom can an Indian presume to speak for his own tribe, much less for another tribe. So what I tell you is my personal understanding as a Cheyenne/Lakota. As you will sometimes hear us say, "Step in another tipi and you may hear another story."

I know what you mean, Grandfather. I asked Tommy whether the Lakota believe in reincarnation, and he laughed. There's no set doctrine, he told me, and different Lakota have different beliefs.

The only three things that are absolutely primary for any Indian are the interrelatedness of all things, the community, and the land. Many people are now familiar with Chief Seath'tl's famous speech in which he says "All things are connected. Whatever befalls the Earth befalls the children of the Earth."

Seath'tl was a Duwamish/Suquamish from the Northwest. Awiakta, a Cherokee from the Southeast, said, "The Creator made the Web of Life and into each strand put the law to govern it. Everything in the universe is part of the web."

Pam Colorado, a present-day Oneida from upstate New York, has stated, "We are related, we are all one. The Indian acknowledges this and so discovers the most liberating aspect of Native science: *life renews*, and all things which support life are renewable."

And, last, the Lakota Holy Man Black Elk from South Dakota said, "Peace . . . comes within the souls of men when they realize their relationship, their oneness, with the Universe and all its powers, and when they realize that at the center of the Universe dwells *Wakan Tanka,* and that this center is really everywhere. It is within each of us."

The contemporary Lakota, Vine Deloria, sums up this innate spirituality beautifully in his book *God is Red* when he writes:

> The relationships that serve to form the unity of nature are
> of vastly more importance to most tribal religions. The Indian
> is confronted with a beautiful Earth in which all things and

experiences have a role to play. The task of the tribal religion, if such a religion can be said to have a task, is to determine the proper relationship that the people of the tribe must have with other living things and to develop the self-discipline within the tribal community so that man acts harmoniously with other creatures. The world that he experiences is dominated by the presence of power, the manifestation of life energies, the whole life-flow of a creation. Recognition that the human being holds an important place in such a creation is tempered by the thought that they are dependent on everything in creation for their existence . . . the awareness of the meaning of life comes from observing how various living things appear to mesh to provide a whole tapestry.

That's certainly a different point of view than Western theology teaches, Grandfather. I studied the work of contemporary Harvard theologian Harvey Cox, who is really a remarkable man. But in his book The Secular City, *when speaking of the Christian tradition, he wrote about that time, just after creation, when Adam was given the responsibility of naming the animals. His words struck me at the time. And if I remember correctly, he said that man is their "master and commander," and that "it is his task to subdue the Earth." Deloria uses the words* unity, *proper relationship,* harmoniously *and* dependent, *whereas Cox uses the words* master, commander, *and* subdue. *I can see how these two worldviews reveal a completely different spirituality.*

Let me tell you a story about something that happened about 30 years ago, though it could have happened at any time in our history. A group of elders gathered in this very tipi. There was an Onondaga from upstate New York, a Choctaw from Mississippi, a Ute from the mountains of Colorado, a Pueblo from New Mexico, and a Miwok from the northern Californian coast. We were all old men at the time. There was not a one who was born in this century.

Long into the night, around a glowing campfire, each related the creation story of his particular tribe, while the others listened with great respect and silence. Being the host, I was the last to speak. When I was finished, we all agreed. But, what did we agree upon? Simply this, Grandson—that it was wonderful how the Creator had provided for each of us. How loving it was for The Great Mysterious to speak to each of us in a way that we could understand, in a way that related to each of our particular circumstances, and, most important, to the land on which we lived.

I remember the old Miwok saying to the Ute when the Ute finished his story, "Brother, how wonderful it is that the Creator has provided for your people in such a beautiful way and brought you here with such grandeur. How blessed we all are!"

What a great story! Even in my own family, and we are all Episcopalians, religion is a topic that creates endless bickering. It's usually chaos at Christmas and Easter when we gather, Grandfather, and the topic of religion comes up. Last year my mother threw up her hands in disgust and said that she didn't want either religion or politics discussed at the table. And if chaos describes what happens within my own family, just think about the problems that so often come up when people of different religions get together to discuss their beliefs.

Did you know that in the United States there are over 500 sects of Christians alone, and many of them think that their path is the only right path to God? I mean, the Catholics argue with the Protestants; and among the Protestants, the Episcopalians argue with the Baptists, and so on. The Jehovah's Witnesses think that they are the only sect that has figured things out, and others tell disrespectful "knock knock" jokes about the Witnesses who go door to door trying to convert people. We have so much to learn from one another, and I am so glad that 44 million Americans are in that learning process. But we still have a very long way to go.

Our people do not argue about religion. Like our Earth, The Great Mysterious speaks in many ways, and not always the same to different peoples. For us, no tribal history or religion is in any way more primary, more accurate, or more truthful than any other. Each and every one is the cumulative experience of the tribe with the Divine in themselves and in the world. And as Chief Seath'tl said, "Our religion is the tradition of our ancestors—the dreams of our old men, given them in the solemn hours of the night by the Great Spirit, and the visions of our sachems—and is within the hearts of our people."

I can see a time in the future when Western culture will view different belief systems with that kind of respect. As a Christian, I believe totally and completely in Jesus' message of love. That we should love our Creator, and love our neighbors as ourselves. And I've learned that this message came through Jesus, a rabbi, because it is also the basis of Judaism. It's always been hard for me to reconcile this message with the realities of history—the cruelty of the Crusades, the Inquisition, the damage done to your culture and so many others by missionaries and evangelical preachers, although some of them were really good people who only wanted to help.

When I think of the war between the Protestants and Catholics in Ireland, the extermination of Jews and others in Nazi Germany, and even the fighting for missionary space in South America and on your reservations, I can see that religion has too often been a roadblock to spirituality rather than a bridge. I'll pray for a time when there's not only religious tolerance, but a lively interest in what each religion has to teach us about living with respect and in right relationship. And I'll pray for the time when all human beings put these teachings into action.

Many contemporary religious leaders are exceptional individuals who are trying to bring people back to the respect of which you speak. They offer messages like that of Wabasha, a Lakota chief of the 18th century. His words were wise: "If any man do anything, sincerely believing that thereby he is worshiping the Great Spirit, he is worshiping the Great Spirit, and his worship must be treated with respect, so long as he is not trespassing on the rights of others."

I have also seen much that is both good and marvelous about Western history and thought. Grandfather Commanda's wampum belts spoke of the possibility that a great culture could be created if the White man came in peace to the Indians, and both cultures could learn from one another. That prophecy did not come to pass initially, but perhaps it is not too late. We may have time yet to create a true Integral Culture, though I daresay that no one of us can yet know what that would look like, only that it would be based on spiritual values.

Each person must commune with The Great Mysterious in the depths of his or her own heart and experience. And make no mistake, that communion is the necessary step to saving this world. As you have said, Grandson, the entire economic system of the world is so interconnected and delicately balanced that change seems impossible. For humans alone it may be. But for The Great Mysterious, all things are possible.

All things seem possible when we believe, Grandfather. But so many people in my culture are so disheartened and stressed by the pressures of the world that we believe only what we are told. And what we are usually told is either bad news or something that takes the magic out of life. You have taught me that spirituality is embodied—it is in the senses and in our relation to the natural world. But modern life even denies our own senses. I was reading a newspaper article about a woman who had poisoned her son, brother, husband, father, and fiancé. In each case, over time, she added arsenic to their food until they became sick and died. They weren't all murdered at once, but over a period of years.

And she made a lot of money off the death of each victim. In the article the chief investigator stated, "I know it is ridiculous, but I could feel the evil in that woman. It was really eerie, but ridiculous, of course."

Now at face value, most people wouldn't see anything wrong with his comment. But think about it, Grandfather. This man was so concerned with not appearing strange that he labeled his own felt experience ridiculous.

Feeling evil is simply not acceptable for a reasonable 20th-century person, Grandson. The entire wisdom of your embodied intuition is cast aside, and much of spirituality with it. Yet in less than a week here, you have learned that it is primarily through the body that we relate to The Great Mysterious and the natural world, not through scientific laws. Let me give you a simple example. Describe to me your experience of the red on this drum.

Well, it's a haunting shade, a dark hue, not bright. It reminds me of fall, of the Earth falling asleep. It's what we would call an unsaturated color. If I had a physics textbook, I could tell you the structure of red light in terms of its waves and clearly delineate it from the other colors of the spectrum. I could also tell you how the light wave reflects off the object into my retina, through the optic nerve to my brain. And I imagine that a neuroscientist could pretty much pinpoint the activity in the brain where the experience is occurring. Perhaps he could even show me a PET scan of the experience.

But you still would not have red from all those data, would you? Suppose that you had never seen any colors before and suddenly by some marvelous operation, or a marvelous healing by a medicine carrier, your full sight was restored. You are lying there having your first experience of a color-full world, and I come up to you as your physical therapist and say, "Mr. Pearson, I am going to teach you your colors. Let us start with red. Red is the least refracted light wave on the spectrum, and it has such and such a wavelength. To further help you, here is a PET scan picture of a brain that is experiencing red. Now let us move on to yellow."

You would be totally lost no matter how much you knew. The experience of red simply cannot be reduced or equated with a physical and biological description. Your mind will never be able to reproduce what your body knows. You mentioned that red reminded you of fall, and I bet that a whole flood of memories and feelings accompanied that perception.

I see what you mean, Grandfather. My experience of red is much more multidimensional than visual pathways. But the body as a way of knowing sure isn't valued by modern science. When I studied psychology, the behaviorists wanted to abolish the whole idea of feelings that they thought were an epiphenomenon—that is, something secondary to and derived from—the basic response that an organism makes to a stimulus. They even want to do away with the idea of consciousness. I'm afraid that's a terrible example of putting Descartes before the horse, if you'll pardon the pun.

I like your sense of humor, Grandson. But the attempt of the behaviorists that you mentioned, to disavow feeling, is very dangerous because it cuts us off from the Circle of Life. We are more than isolated nervous systems responding to stimuli. Taking shelter as a response to a downpour is more than a behavioral event. It is an emotional epiphany.

If we see through the eye of the heart, as well as through the physical eye, we experience gratitude to The Great Mysterious for the moisture that creates life, for the legs to run, for the delight in holding our faces up to the sky, and catching the water on our tongues. We sense the many lifeforms around us celebrating the rain, and our heart opens into holiness. *Mitakuye Oyasin.* Through the rain we sense all our relations. What is not passed by the eye of heart, my Grandson, is only half real.

I think that anyone can understand that the rose you dissect in the botany laboratory is a far cry from the one you pick for your sweetheart. It's the intention behind the giving that's most important. And yet many scientists still have a hard time recognizing that distinction.

For example, so many people have had life-changing responses to a near-death experience in which they seem to rise up out of their body, meet a loving light, and then review their lives in terms of their relationships to other people. Were they loving or not? That's the primary question. And most people return from such an experience with a true intention to be loving toward others. Yet many scientists insist that these experiences aren't objectively real, that they are the result of a lack of oxygen to the brain and that you can dissect the brain and find the pathways responsible—so that the experiences themselves are without any basis in reality and therefore meaningless.

But it seems to me that those kinds of experiences are the essence of reality. After all, I wouldn't be here if it hadn't been for the emotional impact of the dream I had underneath Grandfather Willow. That dream changed the course of my life. What could be more real than that? I know that the natural world was speaking to me, but there are lots of people I'd never mention it to. They'd think I was nuts.

I will read you something that Pam Colorado once said in a speech:

> For a Western educated audience the notion of a tree with spirit is a difficult concept to grasp . . . the universe is alive. Therefore, to see a Native speaking with a tree does not carry

the message of mental instability; on the contrary, this is a scientist engaged in research!

Tatanga Mani, or Walking Buffalo, of the Stoney Assiniboine people said much the same thing:

> We saw the Great Spirit's work in almost everything: sun, moon, trees, wind, and mountains. Sometimes we approach the Great Spirit through these things. Did you know that trees talk? Well, they do. I have learned a lot from trees: sometimes about the weather, sometimes about animals, sometimes about the Great Spirit.

So, you see, Grandson, you are not alone. Grandfather Willow chose well in you. The spiritual relationship to nature as sacred, alive, and in constant communication is at the basis of our ceremonial religious life. Every emotion and thought brought forth by ceremony is felt in our bodies and seared into our consciousness. What anthropologists might reduce to trance or possession, we experience as wholeness—wholeness with our Grandmother Earth, wholeness with all our brothers and sisters, wholeness with the animal spirits, wholeness with the Above Beings, and oneness with The Great Mysterious.

Our ceremony is sacred, Grandson, for it relates each and every member of the community to the whole of creation as it has been experienced by the tribe from the dawn of time. We are present, our ancestors are present, and the whole Earth and The Great Mysterious are present. This history, these ceremonies, bind us together in a kind of community that can only be felt—not described, prescribed, or dissected.

In our religion, the Indian never loses sight of the web of life, or the interconnectedness of all that is. It is part of the religious life to help assure that all is kept in balance and harmony. We are responsible for helping to maintain the integrity and health of our

Grandmother Earth out of respect for the Creator's creation. As the contemporary Onondaga chief Oren Lyons says, this all boils down to respect—respect for the sacredness of Earth and all her children.

You know, Grandfather, I think that people drink and take drugs because, at least for a few minutes, they dissolve the boundaries that keep things separate. The first and only time I smoked marijuana, the grass seemed greener than green, and the bird song seemed to have meaning. I did feel a new respect for the Earth. But then I started to feel cold and shaky, and pretty soon I got paranoid. So I decided that drugs weren't the way to what my culture calls an altered state of consciousness, and what yours calls normal.

I am glad that your drug adventure was not a good one in the end, Grandson. Too many people get trapped by those substances and come to believe that the experience of oneness resides in the drugs rather than in themselves. The sense of oneness that defines spiritual experience is always available, in all situations—not just in what your culture isolates as religious encounters.

Vine Deloria writes: "Religion dominates the tribal culture, and the distinctions existing in Western civilization no longer present themselves." As we have discussed, your civilization is split off into an enormous number of categories. There is the religious and the secular, the political and the social, the business world and home life, and so it goes. But as Deloria continues, "Political activity and religious activity are barely distinguishable. History is not divided into categories. It is simultaneously religious, political, economic, social, and intellectual."

For us there is really no distinction between the daily functioning of the tribe, its customs, and its religion. Spirituality and unity pervade every facet of life. There is no set of values for business, on the one hand, and a different set for another part of life as indicated in such statements as "business is business."

Traditionally, our political system was not seen as separate from our religious responsibilities because the same values apply to every part of life. If it is right from the point of view of the sacred, then it is right and there is no more to say. Laws are not needed to legislate right from wrong.

The other day I said that there was an inverse relationship between law and the spiritual development of a culture. Let me set up a hypothetical and oversimplified case to make the point. Imagine a community based on the ideals of St. Francis and Mother Teresa. Would they need a law to tell them they should not steal? And, if by chance one of them, overcome with a little too much communion wine, took someone else's warm slippers for themselves, what do you think would happen?

Well, given who we are talking about, the guilty party would probably sober up, and in a state of great embarrassment realize what he or she had done and return the slippers. The culprit would more than likely beg for forgiveness and receive it, although they'd be likely to feel bad for some time to come. Or maybe the person whose slippers were stolen would confront the culprit and request that the slippers be given back. In either case, repentance and forgiveness would be the bottom line.

If by some chance the slippers weren't returned, the person would probably be confronted by the community. Public knowledge of the deed would create pressure to think about what happened, which would lead to repentance, and eventually the wayward saint would be reintegrated back into the community.

Now imagine life in a hard-core maximum security prison. Do think there would be much stealing? How about rape, beatings, and occasionally murder? Do you think that many of these people would go to great lengths to get what they could from the system, from each other, or from compromised guards? Would it be conceivable that they would even plan robberies and murders in prison to be executed in the outside world?

That's a no-brainer, Grandfather. Of course they would.

Now is it not the case that these people are going to be subjected to an enormous number of rules and their behavior closely monitored?

Naturally, that's what prisons are about—limiting the freedom and the rights of the inmates because they don't know how to behave ethically and responsibly. They break laws, they hurt people, and they take and destroy other people's property.

In light of your description, Grandson, do you think there is much spirituality among these people?

Among some of them there may be great spirituality. I remember a letter from one prisoner whom Tommy corresponds with. It brought tears to my eyes. He viewed the prison as a kind of monastery in which he was finding his relationship to God and helping others heal. But I know what you're talking about. In general, in a prison situation, people who have been seriously harmed since childhood experience even more brutality. Spirituality is choked out rather than brought forth.

So, on a scale of 1 to 10, would you agree that in terms of spiritual growth, responsibility to the community, conscience, and just plain old human decency, that the first community could be rated as a 10 and the second as a 1? Is it fair to say that our sainted Christian community, in which all of the members are trying to follow the pure, untainted teachings of Jesus to the best of their abilities, does not need any legal rules outside of the community to govern them?

Your point is pretty obvious, Grandfather. The community of prisoners can't function without a set of rigid and enforceable rules and laws. It would be complete chaos without them, whereas for the saintly group it makes no sense to have them.

It seems to me that all societies fall somewhere along a continuum between the two we discussed, that is between 1 and 10. The closer the society is to 1, the more law and regulation it needs. The closer to 10, the less it needs. After all, most laws are a means to protect the members of a society from each other and to ensure some social stability. The 17th-century philosopher Thomas Hobbes described life as "nasty, brutish and short." The Bible portrays humankind as fallen and therefore as basically evil. Indian culture thinks a different way. We see every human being as part of a good and beneficent creation. It is no wonder that Western culture has needed to produce so much law to protect the people from one another, and sadly the law can be used to oppress as well as to protect.

Many groups, such as the Native American Church, are still fighting for their religious freedom, and some ceremonies are still disrupted by government agents. In two Supreme Court decisions, *Lyng* in 1988 and *Smith* in 1990, the United States government refused to protect Indian sacred sites, burial grounds, and other spiritually important lands. Instead, they were opened up to exploitation and development.

Let me read you a little about this, Grandson: Most observers of the Supreme Court were simply confounded at the majority's conclusion that suggested that destroying religion "did not unduly burden it and that no constitutional protections were available to the Indians."

When I used to hear things like that, Grandfather, I would start to question my decision to be a lawyer. And yet we can't give up on systems that are inherently good just because they some-

times serve injustice. I think I can work within the system to use it well, because the law is like a tool. The results depend on who is using it. In any sector, the more voices that speak out against intolerance of any kind, the faster we will reach that spirituality of respect and mutual learning that a new era promises.

Grandson, I know that you value your legal system, but I object to the notion that it is inherently good. A culture that is not corrupt morally and spiritually has no need of a legal system, and one that is, spawns a legal system that is similarly subject to corruption. More important, it is the handmaiden of an economic and social system that is destroying the Earth and its people. And in the case of my own people and other minorities, the law has often been used as an agent of oppression and destruction.

Unfortunately, the way things are, we really do need the law. A Jesuit missionary named Father A. M. Beede came to our Lakota Standing Rock Reservation in 1887. He was filled with youthful enthusiasm for his task, which was to convert us. In 1912 he met with Ernest Thompson Seton, the founder of the Boy Scouts and a true, compassionate friend of the Red man. In a conversation between them, he admitted to Seton that our medicine lodges were "a true Church of God, and we have no right to stamp it out."

Some 15 years later, Seton went back with some students to visit and talk with Father Beede. He was not to be found anywhere at the mission. Seton persevered and finally found him at the reservation. But, he was no longer Father Beede; he was "Lawyer Beede." Seton was very curious and wanted an explanation for this radical change. Beede was just as anxious to offer one.

He told Seton:

> I realized that the Sioux were worshipers of the true God, and their religion was one of truth and kindness. They do not need a missionary, but they do need a lawyer to defend them in the Courts. So I abandoned my role as a missionary and stud-

ied law. After some years I was admitted to the bar of North Dakota, and am their permanent official advocate in all cases involving Indians that come into Court. Of course the missionaries have unfrocked me, and the Indian agents hate me. The Indians can pay me little or nothing for my services. I live in a little cabin built by myself and cook my own meals. But I glory in the fact that I am devoting the last of my days and my strength to the service of this noble, downtrodden Race.

Now that is what I call redemption, a true story of *metanoia*, or change of heart. Spirit works in wondrous ways to bind us together in common cause. And Beede was not the only Christian to admire Indian spirituality and learn from it. Tom Newcomb lived with the Lakota at the time of His Crazy Horse. He told Seton and "dictated for the record" the following:

> I tell you I never saw more kindness or real Christianity anywhere. The poor, the sick, the aged, the widows and the orphans were always looked after first. Whenever we moved camp, someone took care that the widows' lodges were moved first and set up first. After every hunt, a good-sized chunk of meat was dropped at each door where it was most needed. I was treated like a brother; and I tell you I have never seen any community of church people that was as truly Christian as that band of Indians.

If my culture can find a way to treat strangers like brothers, which after all, is a major tenet of Western theology as well as Indian, perhaps we can bring about that new Integral Culture that Paul Ray talks about. But to treat someone like a brother means to respect their beliefs, no matter what they may be, as long as they are not harmful to others. Overcoming judgmentalness is a hard thing to do, Grandfather. I saw a camper the other day with a bumper sticker that read, "I am not color blind," and another that said "Get rid of the queers," and a whole assortment of stickers

*about Jesus as savior and abortion as murder. Religion and intol-
erance are too often linked, but I guess I can think of that the same
way I think of the law. Intolerance is less the fault of religions than
of the people practicing them, and change has to start within the
system, person by person, and of course within the clergy.*

*And truthfully, Grandfather, although I think of myself as a
tolerant person, I can also be pretty judgmental. Sometimes I
look at how a person is dressed, or what they say, and I immediately leap to conclusions about them. I'm not gullible, and I don't
intend to lose my discrimination about people who are untrust-
worthy or dangerous, but I am going to notice my judgments and
try to let go of them.*

Think of a future, Grandson, where people would look upon
one another with a true desire to see the best and to bring it out.
We tend to do what people expect of us. If children get the idea
that they are bad or unworthy, their actions begin to reflect that
judgment. But if they get the idea that they have a gift to offer the
family of humankind, then the gift begins to surface along with
the urge to offer it. A heart of service is born. The same is true for
many adults. When treated with respect, hidden talents emerge
and happiness comes in its wake.

*You've given me a great idea, Grandfather. I love it when a
stranger catches my eye and smiles at me. That can really make
your day. When I leave here, I'm going to make it a practice—I
mean, a real committed spiritual practice, to try to catch people's
eyes and smile at them. Such a simple act seems pretty lame compared to what we'll need to do to save this planet and bring His
Crazy Horse's vision into being, but it's a small step.*

The small steps are key, Grandson, for if we let ourselves
become numb or immobilized by the size of the task before us,
nothing will change and it will soon be too late. But every jour-

ney begins with a single step, and each step we take brings a new horizon into view. I am not one who thinks the world can change with a smile or a prayer, but neither do I underestimate the power of such deeds. They can help us wake up and take committed action to save the environment and to oppose special interests that would take the rain forests down for profit or pollute our Grandmother Earth. In my 118 years, I have learned never to underestimate the power of love. It is the very face of the Mystery.

⊗　　⊗　　⊗

CHAPTER SEVEN

VALUES:
TEACH THE CHILDREN WELL

Chasing Deer shook John awake well before sun-up. "Grandson, get dressed and come right away. Our fox friend has had pups."

"How do you know, Grandfather? It's the middle of the night," John whispered from behind the veil of sleep, rubbing his eyes.

"She called to me in a dream. She's had two girl pups. Come and let us visit the new family."

John was dubious. "Wouldn't she be happier if we left her alone? I thought that wild animals didn't like people intruding on their nests."

"She's been intruding on yours, if you see it that way, all week. The least you can do is return the favor."

So the two men picked their way through the pitch-dark night, the moon covered by a thick layer of clouds. Chasing Deer moved with grace, anticipating and sidestepping every branch and stone. It was as if his feet had eyes. John followed him warily, asking the old man to slow down.

"Just focus your intention on the joy of visiting Sister Fox, rather than on your fear of stumbling, Grandson. Your body will find the way naturally."

After a few minutes, they arrived at the rock outcropping under which the fox had made her den. Chasing Deer asked John to sit down a respectful distance from her nest, and he began to sing. In a few minutes, a dark form appeared at the entrance to the den. It was the mother fox. In her mouth she held a mewling pup. She brought it over to Chasing Deer and dropped the baby in his lap. A minute later, she appeared with her other girl pup. Chasing Deer continued his strange song, and both pups fell asleep in the warm circle of his arms. The mother fox joined in the singing, her voice as reedy as the wind.

John sat in perfect silence as they finished chanting the ancient melody and the fox took her babies, one by one, back to the warmth of her den.

※ ※ ※

John: Visiting the fox and her cubs was the most magical experience I've ever had, Grandfather. I will always remember the song that you sang, and how she joined her voice with yours.

Chasing Deer: It was I that joined my voice with hers, Grandson. Her great-great grandmother taught me that song many years ago, and through it the fox and I became one. Her family was my family. In my childhood, I was trained to harmonize with the natural world and to listen to the voice of the winds, the trees, the animals, the stones, the body, and the spirit beings as they speak through dreams, ceremonies, and synchronicities.

My people say that we have three eyes—the physical organs that see, the eye of the mind, and the eye of the heart. All three work together: perceptual experience, thoughts and knowledge, and good feelings of harmony. To deny any of them—what we see, what we think, or how we feel—is to be headed for trouble. Action is most skillful when all three eyes work together. So we must think, pray, and feel with the depths of our whole being before acting on anything that is not perfectly clear.

My world is more impulsive, Grandfather. We want answers yesterday. I've made a lot of mistakes by acting hastily without checking that those three eyes had the same focus. There was a girl named Julie who I met at the end of my freshman year. We dated steadily most of the way through college. She was absolutely gorgeous, lots of fun, very bright, from a great family, and my parents loved her. They thought she'd be a good match and started to kid us about when we were getting engaged.

Although I liked her—I even thought I loved her—and there was great chemistry, her values were different from mine. She kept talking about how she wanted to live in a grand house, have elegant parties and all, and I was thinking that if we got married, I'd be a slave to her needs. I started to feel anxious and worried, but everyone else was totally invested in our being the perfect couple.

In the middle of senior year, the pressure was starting to get to me. I figured that she was a nice person and that we might as well get engaged. So we did, even though my heart told me not to. We were supposed to be married right after graduation—just about now, in fact. But when our mothers started to make out the guest list I panicked and broke off the engagement. I hurt Julie and a lot of other people because I acted impulsively, trying to please our families and friends, even though my three eyes weren't in harmony.

I am glad that you were able to follow your heart, Grandson, for choosing a mate is one of the most important decisions a human being can make. A simple yes or no can change your life forever. Good and respectful answers take much time. That is why there are so many long pauses in conversation when the old Indians speak with each other. We do not feel the need to answer right away. It is disrespectful, for it shows that you have probably not taken the time to really hear and understand the other person. We are in no hurry. Efficiency knows a time schedule; skillful living does not.

By acting only when the eyes of the mind and heart are one, much of the guilt that plagues people can be avoided. Guilt like you felt about Julie. The correspondence between thought and being is natural to my culture. But then, I was raised in a time and circumstance where I was not split to pieces with a thousand and one internal and external demands, as many people are in this time.

Do you think that it's impossible to be whole when life is so fast-paced and you feel busy and pressured? I'm worried about that, Grandfather. It seems that everyone I talk to is constantly complaining about all their responsibilities and having so little time for themselves.

Anyone can be whole, Grandson, if you make a point—I would even say, a discipline—of putting time aside for yourself. I know this is difficult for modern people, but without it the stress of life becomes like a roaring wind full of dust that blinds the eye of the heart. Unskillful decisions are made, and the stress mounts. Here in the United States, heart disease is the number-one cause of death, and stress is one of the largest contributors. In Japan they even have a word for death from overwork.

Learn to take time out from the "busyness" of doing to reflect deeply and to let life speak to you, Grandson. Especially if you feel confused—that is a good time to go away by yourself. Rest from the external pressures that cloud your vision. Seek the solace of nature. Many times we already know the answers we seek, but the chatter of the mind prevents them from surfacing. And the Above Beings speak to us with good counsel, but without a quiet heart we cannot hear. Wisdom is available to everyone, but unlike knowledge, it cannot be learned. It is received through the open heart, the quiet mind. This, I expect, is why one of your

Ten Commandments specifies a weekly Sabbath to rest, renew, and celebrate life. But how many people actually take a Sabbath day every week, or a Sabbath year every seven sun returns?

I don't think my father's had a real day of rest for years, Grandfather. And he's proud of it. Busyness has become like a badge of honor. It makes people feel important. I love my father, and I feel concerned for him because I don't think he's really happy. There are always too many demands on him, and a smile is a pretty rare thing. He's most relaxed when we go to Briarley in the summer, but even there he takes a briefcase full of work. I know that he loves me very much, but I wish we had more time to spend together. Work is really the center of his life.

The pressures of business and finance are very real for your father, Grandson. And also for many women in modern times. What of the single mothers who must work to provide for their children financially, and yet do not have the time to provide for them emotionally because they are not home enough? You grieve the time you were denied with your father, and so it is for many children who grieve the absence of parents. There are other griefs in a money-centered culture as well—griefs that are more subtle. For example, Grandson, the true nature of the human heart is generosity and the desire to give, but even for the most compassionate person in the modern world, giving is not always possible.

Here is a simple example. Your neighbor develops a severe kidney ailment and desperately needs a transplant. He is out of work due to downsizing, has no medical insurance, and nobody wants to hire a 58-year-old man. So, he comes to you with his plight. Either he raises $150,000 or he dies. You have $200,000 in your retirement account. But if you take it out to help your friend, not only will you lose the chance to retire, but the government will penalize you for early withdrawal!

You are faced with a terrible dilemma. If you help your friend, you put yourself and your family in a grave financial position from which you may not recover. On the other hand, if you do not help save your friend, then he dies and his family suffers. So, you are faced with an agonizing decision in which harm is going to occur no matter what you decide. This entire situation has occurred because of the centrality of economic values. The individual is like an atom, and the family a molecule at best, split off from the tissue of others and the organism of the world. In our culture as it once was, each member of the tribe was as important as any other. If one was hungry, all were hungry.

You've told me that we can't all go back to the old ways of your culture, Grandfather. But in knowing about them, I think we'll have a much better chance of forming the Integral Culture that Paul Ray talks about. I mean, isn't that the point of understanding other cultures? That they inspire you, give you ideas, and remind you of things you'd forgotten? And if there's a Purification, then maybe the survivors will be forced to live in a way where the old knowledge will become immediately important.

Well, should that time ever come, John, maybe they will call you the Receiver of Memories. Perhaps the most important things to remember are generosity and love for the children. The Indian cultures were boundlessly generous, and at celebrations like weddings we often still have giveaways in which the young couple give their most prized possessions away to the guests. But others give back to them, so that goodness is experienced by all. At times in our generosity we may suffer temporary discomfort, but it is not worthy of mention compared to the joy of giving.

An old Winnebago said:

You take something of yourself and give it free of charge.
You take a part of yourself and do so because you believe you

are connected to everything else. You become aware of yourself as a part of everything. You suffer momentarily so that
someone else will not have to.

A Winnebago lesson for the children went as follows:

> Try to do something for your people—something difficult.
> Have pity on your people and love them. If a man is poor, help
> him. Give him and his family food, give them whatever they
> ask for. If there is discord among your people, intercede. Take
> your sacred pipe and walk into the midst. Die if necessary in
> your attempt to bring about reconciliation.

So many of the worries, so many of the heartaches, so many
of the seemingly unfair decisions that people of goodwill in your
culture have to make did not arise for a tribal people where we
were trained from childhood that we were all one body.

*Children are so important, Grandfather, since they're truly our
future. If our culture is going to change, it will be because of the values we raise our children with. Even when I was young, kids were
raised with more respect for their elders and the Earth than they
have today. My mother read me Dr. Seuss stories—he was a great
environmentalist, you know. I'll send you a copy of* The Lorax,
*which my mother must have read to me at least a hundred times.
The Lorax is kind of a nature spirit who speaks for the trees that are
being cut down to make "thneeds," a useless item that everyone
"needs." Eventually the trees are all gone, except for a single seed
that is entrusted to a little boy by the Onceler, the bad guy who cut
all trees down and recognizes the error of his ways too late.*

*My younger cousins don't get read to as much as I did.
They're growing up on a steady stream of violent TV shows and
movies. On the average, kids now see 20,000 acts of TV violence
before the age of 17, and unfortunately they adjust to it as the
norm of the culture.*

If there is going to be hope for the world and the children, Grandson, televisions need to be turned off most of the time. Books are wonderful because they train the imagination. And good stories like you tell me Dr. Seuss has written become part of the values of a child, particularly when a parent or other elder takes the time to relate the story to real-life events and refer back to them over and over again. The closeness that a parent and child experience during storytelling is an important part of the growth process, a part that the television can never supply.

But the love and training of our children actually begins with conception. From the time that the Lakota mother knows that there is a new life growing inside her, she begins to nurture the child not only physically, but spiritually, and as a future member of the tribe. In the old days, and even for traditionals now, the pregnant woman spends much time in silence and meditation.

Let me read to you from Ohiyesa, also called Charles Alexander Eastman, the first Indian ever to go to medical school. Eventually he returned to his people and to the old ways because he felt that they were much superior to those of his adopted White culture. He says of the expectant mother, "Her attitude and secret meditations must be such as to instill into the receptive soul of the unborn child the love of the Great Mystery and a sense of kinship with all creation." She concentrates and visualizes the traits that she admires among the members of her band, sending them through her thoughts to her unborn.

In the old days, our women generally had their babies alone in nature. There were seldom complications, and if you read the writings of the White men who were in contact with us before our destruction, you will read of their amazement that shortly after birth our women were back at their chores. The recordings of the French Recollect priest, Chrestien Le Clercq, about the Indians he lived with in Canada during the last part of the 17th century, are not uncommon.

He writes:

> They are accouched with very great ease, and carry heavy burdens during their pregnancy. Some indeed finding themselves overtaken by this illness in going to fetch wood, retire a little apart in order to bring the child into the world and they carry the wood to the wigwam upon their backs, with the new born babe in their arms, as if nothing at all had happened. An Indian woman, when in a canoe one day, feeling herself pressed by the pains of childbirth, asked those of her company to put her on shore, and to wait for her a moment. She entered alone into the woods, where she delivered a baby boy; she brought him to the canoe, which she helped to paddle all the rest of the journey.

According to my mother, childbirth was the worst pain she's ever experienced, although she also said it was the most beautiful, holy moment of her life. I suppose that Indian women must have been in much better physical condition if childbirth was so easy. These days it gets treated like an illness that the woman won't survive without proper medical attention.

Think back to what I just read, Grandson. Even in the 17th century, pregnancy and birth were thought of as an illness in your culture. But that is the distancing from nature once again. I do wonder about one thing. The Bible says that bearing children in pain would be Eve's punishment for eating the fruit of the Tree of Knowledge and defying God. Perhaps since Indians did not know that story and had no fear of birth-pain as the wrath of an angry God, they did not feel so much pain. After all, the mind and body are not separate. They are one. What we believe becomes the very substance of our cells.

In the old times, our children were born naturally and lovingly upon the Earth. Most children nowadays are born in the sterile, cold, and I would even say, abusive circumstances of the modern hospital.

Most of the women of my mother's generation would have been terrified of a home birth, Grandfather, even though their grandmothers often delivered in their own beds. But a lot of women are now choosing home births, or at least births in hospital "birthing rooms" that are relatively natural and nontechnical. They can even bring their children with them to witness the birth of the new baby. I would say that this is progress, and another example of how the wisdom of our grandmothers turns out to be validated by modern science.

This is a very hopeful trend, Grandson. The state of California launched a study in 1979 seeking to find the roots of violence in American society. Three years later, the results were in. The report stated that "the first and foremost cause of the epidemic increase of violence in America was the violence done to infants and mothers at birth."

My mother tells the story of how, even though my birth was normal, I was pulled out with forceps. Apparently my head was squashed and I looked terrible for a week. Her doctor actually said that if the birth was natural, I'd be more likely to lose IQ points from the long journey down the birth canal. Can you believe that? As if squeezing an infant's head with forceps wouldn't damage the brain, or as the study you just read suggests, even the ability to bond that's so crucial to reducing violence.

The harm to modern children does not end with the birth process. Most are not breast fed, as if science, rather than Grandmother Earth, knows what is best for a child. Let me read you a report published in December, 1997 in the prestigious *British Medical Journal.* I am going to read you the whole thing, which would really be quite humorous were it not so sad. As if we need studies to prove that women have breasts for a very good reason.

Here it is:

Mothers should breast feed for at least the first year of an infant's life because of the health benefits for both the baby and mother, says the American Academy of Pediatrics. In a new policy statement, published in the December issue of the journal *Pediatrics*, the academy said that studies conducted in industrialized countries have shown that breast feeding can decrease the incidence or severity of conditions such as diarrhoea, ear infections, and bacterial meningitis. The research has also shown that breast feeding may offer protection against sudden infant death syndrome, insulin dependent diabetes, and allergic diseases, among others. Breast feeding reduces the mother's risk of ovarian and pre-menopausal breast cancer. It can also save a family more than $400 on the cost of infant formula during the first year of life and reduce parental absence from work due to child illness. However, only 21% of women in the United States breast feed at six months.

At this rate, they'll probably discover that pure water and clear air also benefit mothers and babies. But seriously, Grandfather, pollution is an enormous problem for children and nursing mothers. A study published in the late 1970s that I read in my environmental science course reported that 50 percent of all women tested had pollutants called polychlorinated biphenyls, or PCBs, in their milk in concentrations so high that it was deemed unfit for human consumption. And more recent studies have linked PCBs with violence, hyperactivity, and lower IQs. So, what are we to do? The cows' milk that goes into formulas is also polluted, so I suppose that breast feeding is still best. But what we really need to do is to clean up the environment before the children turn into killer mutants.

You are right, of course, Grandson. The children must be protected. But it is not just their birth and feeding that we must think about. It is also their nurturing and the values they are raised with. Although women must be able to work in the world and be free to offer their gifts, it cannot be at the expense of the children. It is best if one or the other parent stays at home with the little ones, even if that means less income. Day-care centers vary greatly in the care they provide, but none can substitute for the tender love of a parent. We have to ask why so many children are killing themselves, why they are turning to drugs and alcohol at younger and younger ages. And why we hear more and more terrible stories of children killing one another, which as you may recall was one of the Zuni prophecies that was a harbinger of the final days.

One time I was at my house on the reservation meeting with a group of elders. A meeting had been called by a BIA social worker. She was concerned, so she said, about the poverty among our children. We listened politely. When she was done, old Matt Yellowhawk said to her, "If you want to know what real poverty is, I'll tell you. It is a child sitting in front of a television set in a large suburban home all alone while the parents are sipping cocktails at some social function. Now that is poverty!"

I really admire my mother because she didn't let me watch much TV, and I know it's tempting to use the box, as we call it, as a baby-sitter. I read a lot, and she read to me and told me stories that her mother had told her. I played make-believe, especially with space figures—and you'll get a kick out of this—cowboys and Indians. I also spent a lot of time outdoors collecting bugs and trying to start fires with a magnifying glass—not actually to set anything on fire, but just to see if it could be done. My mother let me be curious, and I'm appreciating her more and more as I grow older.

That is good, Grandson, for a mother gives so much to her children. A grateful child is a pleasure to her and a comfort all her life. One of the things that our mothers trained us to do early on was to enjoy silence. To be able to sit still for long periods. This technique was used to sharpen the senses. We would concentrate on what we were hearing, seeing, smelling, and feeling. This was most enjoyable. I loved to enter the stillness and tune in to the small voices of the insects and animals, the trees, and the grass. They spoke to me so that I never felt alone or bored. This is why the fox and I can sing together. To us, a restless child would be one who was not properly developed. There is plenty both inwardly and outwardly to absorb a child's attention. They should not need to be continually entertained.

I took a ten-week course in meditation last year, Grandfather, which is basically learning to sit in silence and pay attention without any expectations of what's supposed to happen. And boy, were people bored for the first few weeks! Other than realizing how hard it is to keep the mind from continuously thinking, boredom was the single biggest complaint. But gradually, the idea of boredom dissolved when we learned to attend to the subtle movements of the body—the breath, the heartbeat, the flow of energy that is always moving and changing. Little by little we also became more attuned to sounds in the outside world. From a birdsong or a telephone ringing, I learned an important lesson. The birdsong was welcome, interesting. I could incorporate it into the meditation. But the telephone made me irritable because I labeled it as a disturbance. After a while, I got the hang of what the teacher called nonjudgmental awareness, or mindfulness. The song and the phone were the same, just sounds that came into and went out of what she called the "spacious sky of clear mind." The spacious sky was unchanging, open and receptive. It gave me both an experience of, and a metaphor for, peace that have been so valuable. It's also taught me how to pay close attention— something that you learned by sitting still as a child.

Our teacher told a wonderful story that makes a lot of sense now that I know how you were raised. Some army intelligence unit was interviewing applicants. They sat in a waiting room first, and then were questioned by a senior officer. The question was, "Please describe the waiting room in as much detail as possible." One of the applicants, who was an Indian, had a complete sense of the room—the temperature, the smell, the sounds, and the sights, right down to a description of the six pictures on the wall and the fact that one was slightly tilted. He got the job.

That is a good story, Grandson. When you live as part of the natural world, survival depends on what you call mindfulness. The direction that the wind comes from, its fragrance, tell of the weather, of where the animals will be. The world is rich with information that Indian children learn naturally as part of life. How wonderful it would be if this meditation you speak of could be taught to children in schools. They would learn to be more attentive and curious, less judgmental. What you said of your different reaction to the telephone and the birdsong was most astute. So much discomfort is caused by judgment of what is pleasurable and what is not. I had a visitor here early last June, and it snowed on the third day of his time here. This is not uncommon in the mountains. But he was quite upset. It was supposed to be warm and sunny, not cold, wet, white, and muddy. Immediately his mood became morose. Had it been December, I imagine that he would have found the snow most beautiful since it was expected.

In addition to generosity and what you would call mindfulness, Indian children of my day were also raised with reverence for the world and with love as primary values. And as we grew, generosity, courage, and chastity were added. These were the basic values upon which Indian life depended. Our lessons were learned quickly, and by six or seven, a child knew well how to be a Lakota. Learning to be generous started at a very early age, and when our parents performed an act of kindness, we were participants whenever possible.

Let me read to you again, Grandson, from Luther Standing Bear's *Land of the Spotted Eagle*:

> Little children were taught to give and to give generously. A sparing giver was no giver at all. Possessions were given away until the giver was poor in the world's goods and had nothing left but the delight and joy of pure strength . . . When mothers gave food to the weak and the old, they gave portions to their children at the same time so that the children could perform the service of giving with their own hands. Little Lakota children often ran out and brought into the tipi an old and feeble person who chanced to be passing. If a child did this, the mother must at once prepare food. To ignore the child's courtesy would be unpardonable. But it is easy to touch the heart of pity in a child, so the Lakota was taught to give at any and all times for the sake of becoming strong and brave. The greatest brave was he who could part with his most cherished belongings and at the same time sing songs of joy and praise. It was a custom to hold "give away dances" and to distribute presents that were costly and rare. To give is the delight of the Lakota.

I was fortunate, Grandfather, because my family also believed that children should learn to give at an early age. Every year on Thanksgiving, our family goes to a soup kitchen and we all help serve the needy before going home to our family celebration. We do the same on Christmas. My grammar school collected our old clothes for the poor, but also suggested that we use some of our allowance money to buy something new. I used to buy socks all the time and look for sales so that I could buy more. So I was lucky that way.

Like you, our children learned these things by example. And it would be unthinkable to offer a child some reward or prize for doing the right thing. The only reward was doing the good deed.

To equate goodness with receiving anything was considered unhealthy and degrading.

Then it's a good thing that Santa Claus didn't show up in your tipis. I lived in fear that he was watching me all year, seeing if I was bad or good, and that he'd punish me by not showing up or by giving me something that wasn't nice.

That sounds terrible, Grandson. I have never thought that Santa Claus was a very good idea. Gifts given with no strings attached are better for a child's growth, for they speak to him of his own intrinsic worth. We also thought that children developed better if they were spaced more widely than you and your sister. Luther Standing Bear recalls that, "It was a law with the Lakotas that for the first six years of a child's life, it should have the unrestricted care of the mother and that no other children should be born within the six-year period."

We felt that a child deserves the absolute attention and concern of its parents and the tribe during these formative years. And as our children grew, they always had the constant friendship of some elder. It did not always need to be the mother or the father. It might be one of the grandparents, or an aunt or uncle. Each child was a child of the entire band, for we belonged not just to our immediate family, but to the entire tribe.

No matter where we rambled, we were at home, and in every tipi we were treated no differently than in our own. As Standing Bear recalls his childhood:

> And so the days of my infanthood and childhood were spent in surroundings of love and care. In manner, gentleness was my mother's outstanding characteristic. Never did she, nor any of my caretakers, ever speak crossly to me or scold me for failures or shortcomings. For an elder person in the Lakota tribe to strike or punish a young person was an unthinkable

brutality. Such an ugly thing as force with anger back of it was unknown to me, for it was never exhibited in my presence.

And so it was for all our children. Le Clercq observed correctly when he wrote, "One cannot express the tenderness and affection which the fathers and mothers have for their children." The universality of patience and unconditional love of the children is repeatedly mentioned by those who observed Indians in our natural state. The founder of the Boy Scouts, Ernest Thompson Seton, who spent much of his life living and learning from various tribes wrote, "Love of their children is a dominant characteristic of the Red race. I never saw an Indian child spoiled. I never saw an Indian child spanked."

In-the-Middle, an old Mescalero Apache, summed up the wisdom of our people: "If you do bad things, your children will follow you and do the same. If you want to raise good children, be decent yourself." An old Assiniboine tradition says in part that "good acts done for the love of children become stories good for the ears of people. They become as coveted things."

One of the problems when I was growing up was that we spent more time at school than at home, and the teachers were kind of mixed. I had some wonderful people who, when I grow old and look back at my life, will still stand out like beacons. A seventh-grade English teacher, Mr. Tolson, really gave me the confidence to express myself and to write humor and satire. But my first-grade teacher was like an ogre. She kept telling me that I was bad and disruptive, and I was terrified to go to school, so I kept on faking stomachaches. It took months for my mother to catch on and finally have me transferred to another class. So I hated school for years.

Our children were not taught in classrooms as yours are. It was the sacred responsibility of a child's parents to teach him or her all that they knew. While skills were obviously taught, the first and most important emphasis was on character, on being one of the People. The primary emphasis was not on mastery of things, but on mastery of self. This had two sides to it—the full development of each child as an individual and, concomitantly, the full recognition of the rights of every member of the tribe. This is an aspect of tribal life that may be difficult for someone brought up in Western culture to understand. Let me explain.

Our people are highly individualized, yet devoted first and foremost to the community. You see this individuality in our names. Each is different. Names designate something important about the individual, whether it be a trait, an experience, or an accomplishment. For instance, Young-Man-Afraid-of-His-Horses, who lived during the time of His Crazy Horse, had a name that if properly translated meant, "He is such a feared warrior that his enemies are even afraid of his horses."

My name, Chasing Deer, was given to me when I was about 18. I loved to chase deer until we were both exhausted. I would run miles and miles until the deer and I were both so tired that we would lay down and get to know each other. My name was a recognition of great stamina and fleetness of foot. I would play tag with the deer still if I could find one my age!

A name was something to live up to and something that was wholly individualized, and one's name often changed as one's life and experience changed. As a child, His Crazy Horse was known as Light Curly Hair, for the color of his hair, until he proved himself a mighty warrior and his father passed on to him his own name as a mark of honor.

In terms of our individual talents and gifts, our parents did not try to tell us what to do or what to become. Mothers sought only the welfare of their child and the cultivation of the child's own individuality. In your society, children are often thought of as status symbols. If they are smart, go to a good school, and enter a prestigious profession, then that reflects well on the parents. I'll read to you from the Lakota, Luther Standing Bear:

> Today mother-power is weak, scattered to many places—
> taken over by the preacher, nurse, lawyer, and others who
> superimpose their will. This loss applies also to the white
> mother, for she too is blinded and confused by the intricacies
> of the society in which she lives. And the incongruity of it all
> is that the child has not become individualized, but has become
> stamped with the ideas of others. Few today are the youthful
> individual thinkers and doers who dare step out of the ranks
> close about them which try to force them to conform. This
> process was not possible in Lakota society in tribal times. The
> Indian mother pointed the way, but she followed in her son's
> or daughter's path. She did not take from, but rather, added to
> their strength by urging it to express itself.

*I see hopeful signs in the renewal of mother-power, and
father-power as well, Grandfather. There's a growing trend
toward home-schooling and a type of cooperative home-
schooling where kids learn at home three days a week, and whatever parent is teaching them goes with them to school the other
two days. Some parents are paid to act as teachers to coordinate
the lessons, cover the more technical aspects of each subject, and
ensure that the curriculum is followed. I have two cousins who
went to a school like that, and both of them graduated from high
school, passing the New York State Regents exam, at 15. They
weren't pressed to finish, nor did they hurry through. Each went
at her own pace, developing her own special interests. And they
both loved school. My aunt was one of the founding members.*

Grandson, according to the prophecies of many tribes, it will
be the women, the bearers of life, who bring about the great
changes we hope for. So I am not surprised that the majority of
Cultural Creatives, with such a strong interest in education and

community, are women. I have always found it interesting that at a time when there were few women academics, so many of the early writers and defenders of Indian culture were women. We owe a lot to Angie Debo, Mari Sandoz, Frances Densmore, Eve Ball, Helen Hunt Jackson, Elsie Clews Parsons, and others. I think the women, being the givers of life, tuned to relationship and the feminine qualities of nurture, saw and admired these traits in our culture.

Indians know that the strength of the tribe resides in the strength of its women. Did you know that among the Iroquois it was the women, the grandmothers, who decided if war was to be waged? They decided if the lives of the young men should be put at risk, and only if they could see the benefit seven generations into the future did they allow the conflict to occur. It was only right that the givers of life should be given the decision that might destroy it. The grandmothers were also given the power to ask a chief to step down.

Among my mother's people, there is a proverb that speaks to this: "A nation is not conquered until the hearts of its women are on the ground. Then it is done, no matter how brave its warriors or how strong their weapons."

And, an old elder from my father's tribe said, "The honor of the people lies in the moccasin tracks of the women. Walk the good road. . . . Be strong, with the warm, strong heart of the Earth. No people goes down until their women are weak and dishonored, or dead upon the ground. Be strong and sing the strength of the Great Powers within you, all around you."

We must heed women's wisdom, for it is of the Earth, and the relationships between the sacred circles. And we must support the mothers and grandmothers for their own sake, for the welfare of the children, and for the survival of the Earth in this time of choice where the future of the planet hangs in the balance.

166

CHAPTER EIGHT

THE WISDOM OF THE ELDERS:
COMMUNITY AND HAPPINESS

The night sky was filled with stars in the Black Hills, so bright that it seemed to John he could almost reach out and touch them. The silence was as soft as velvet, and if you listened, it had its own sound. The mingled voices of the wind, the stream, and the few crickets who could survive in the arid altitude was so rich that John sat and listened for hours.

During this time, his mind was curiously quiet. Pulled neither into the past nor the future, he found a sense of peace, a kind of center in his own depths. And it occurred to him that he was happy. He stretched his long limbs with deep contentment, rising off the rough bench in front of the cabin, and looking out at the silhouettes of the Tree People in the woods all around him.

The thought crossed his mind that if he had not dreamed of Chasing Deer beneath the limbs of Grandfather Willow, he would be in France already, perhaps watching the girls on the Riviera or admiring the paintings of the old masters in the Louvre. And he startled himself with a peal of laughter that temporarily stunned the crickets into silence. *What better place to be than right here,* he thought. *What a privilege to spend this time with an elder, so wise and gentle.*

John slept deeply that night, the slumber of a child without a care in the world. Once again, he and Chasing Deer arose to greet Grandfather Sun and Wakan Tanka with gratitude for a new day. But by the time they had bathed in the stream and visited Sister Fox and her pups, a familiar anxiety had taken root in John's belly. In a few days, he would be leaving for Europe and then starting law school. He wondered whether he could find his peaceful center in a busy world, and what sort of world he could help create where peace could be a common experience, rather than an epiphany.

John: Your description of child-rearing among your people was very touching, Grandfather. When I was growing up, I had a lot of the same benefits. Mom was home with us kids, but three of our grandparents were also around a lot. My dad's mother died in a car crash when I was a baby, but his father, "Pops," lived close by. He'd pick me up every Saturday, and we'd do something together like go fishing or tie flies.

He took my sister and me camping, too, and that was our favorite thing other than spending the summers at Briarley. We'd gather there with aunts, uncles, cousins, and Mom's folks, and we were really like a little tribe. I can remember hiding under the kitchen table when I was small, listening to the stories that the grown-ups told. It was so exciting, like hearing about another world.

Chasing Deer: Children love stories, Grandson. We all do. They have the power to recreate the past and shape the future. A grandparent or other elder who has lived in accord with the wisdom of the three eyes can tell stories that bring the listener into harmony—stories that guide and heal. As we age and experience both joy and sorrow, victory and defeat, love and loss, the tapestry of our life grows. And at any time we can rise above the tapestry, with all its colors and characters, and perceive a fresh story in its warp and woof. That is the strength of the human heart. It creates meaning, and that meaning touches and teaches others, spreading wisdom.

Or spreading pain. I remember one aunt who was always complaining. Nothing was ever right, and to hear her talk, you'd think the world was a paranoid plot, and everyone and everything—even the weather—was out to get her.

I wonder what kind of stories she heard from her own elders, Grandson. Stories are like templates, these days you might call them software, that are installed in young minds and hearts. They become frameworks in which the growing child can organize his or her experience. And these stories are the most important legacy we give to our young, more important than the skills we teach. Once the basic story of life is in place, Grandson, it is hard to change. That is why a People's creation story is so important. It tells of their relationship to the Creator and the purpose of life.

That's one of the reasons I'm glad that my father let me quit Sunday School. I had a teacher in the fourth grade who loved to tell the creation story from Genesis, but like all storytellers, she embroidered a bit and emphasized the parts that made sense to her. She really got off on evil and the fall from God's grace. She said that the snake in the garden was like an evil urge always lurking in our minds, tempting us to do wrong. And if we listened, we'd go to hell.

She made a serious mistake, Grandson. Why would an elder teach children that their hearts are bad, that they cannot trust themselves? Children flower when they know that the human heart is good, in harmony with *Wakan Tanka*. It is the sacred duty of the elders to teach each child of their goodness and of the history and customs of their religion in a way that brings that innate beauty out. Grandparents played a large role in this in my time. Our old people were the lifeblood of our communities and the most respected members. It seems that elders often do not have proper respect in your culture. How did that come to be, Grandson?

Well, for one thing, the United States is a young country, and its population is also young. I learned in sociology class that back in the 1700s, the average age of an American was only 17. Infant mortality was high. A lot of mothers died in childbirth, and men died young in wars. So there weren't that many elders around. We're still a youth-oriented society, Grandfather, although the average age is climbing every year.

Another reason why elders may not be accorded respect is due to family structure. Eighty-five percent of Americans lived in multigenerational families as recently as the mid-1940s, but by the early 1990s, that figure had dropped to less than 5 percent. When we talk about aging, my mother always laughs and tells me I'm lucky that she has money because I'll never have to take her in when she grows old. She thinks she'd be a burden. Her idea of aging is getting progressively more infirm and draining other people's energy and resources.

In the old days, our elders were hardy like I am. And if a person feels useful, Grandson, they remain hardy much longer. When you have things to do that add to the good of the whole, the life-force continues to flow like a river in your veins. But if a person feels useless, the life-force ebbs. As Luther Standing Bear wrote:

> Parental devotion was very strong and the old were objects of care and devotion to the last. They were never given

cause to feel useless and unwanted, for there were duties performed only by the old and because it was a rigidly kept custom for the young to treat their elders with respect.

Much of the care of the children was left to the grandmother. Being experienced and wise, she was the keeper of the ways of raising children. Young mothers always sought out the grandmother's advice. It is, after all, the rightful place of older women to be teachers, for they are rich in experience. We know that the community is only as strong as its women, and they are greatly respected. Old men also became tribal leaders and teachers whose wisdom was considered a community treasure. Through these grandmothers and grandfathers, thousands of years of tribal experience was passed on from one generation to the next.

Traditional grandparents expected children to be able to repeat exactly what they said. As a result, most Indians had excellent memories. More than one of your leaders was impressed with the Indians' ability to repeat an entire discussion or treaty that occurred years before without missing a word. In the old days, we carried our history in our hearts and minds, not on the pages of books. We knew who we were, where we had been, and what it was to carry forward. Look at the face of any old Indian, and you will see what I mean. He has not the slightest doubt of who he is, what he stands for, and what his responsibilities are. They are etched in his face and in the pulses of his heart.

Yes, a lot of the portraits of the old Indians in your cabin are full of character. There is a strength and dignity there that only seems to increase with age. The elder years seem like a period of fullness in your culture, Grandfather, while they're often thought of as a time of loss in mine. In fact, if I were to tell people that I had spent over a week with a man more than 100 years old, they would probably imagine you as bedridden or senile, rather than as the strong, wise man that you are.

I am sorry for the modern elders and children who lack each other's company. The generations need one another to grow and thrive. Our children were always in the eye of the tribe and the elders. There were few secrets. From the time the village crier announced a birth, most everyone was aware of every developmental step the child took. Each milestone was a cause for celebration. Ohiyesa wrote:

> Not a step in the child's development was overlooked as an excuse to bring it before the public by giving a feast in its honor. Thus the child's progress was known to the whole clan as to a larger family, and the child grew to adulthood with a sense of reputation to sustain.

You see, the tribe as a whole—all the generations together—was both mother and father. We could never move about as you do, leaving our elders and relatives without experiencing the deepest sadness. That is one reason why close to 50 percent of our children sent off to the infamous Indian boarding schools perished. They died of broken hearts and loneliness. In the boarding schools, elders did not respect the children, but called them dirty savages. And the lessons they learned were like those that your Sunday School teacher taught. That they had bad hearts.

I didn't know about the boarding schools before this week, Grandfather. I always thought they were a good thing, a social service that would teach Indian children to rise above the poverty of the reservations and have a better shot at life in modern America. I didn't realize how much had been lost when the community structure was broken down.

I tell you about our families and customs to give you hope. People can and have lived in harmony with each other and with the natural world since they first stepped from the mists of time. You see, Grandson, human beings are tribal animals. They cannot live in isolation without great damage to themselves, without creating violence and suffering. Tommy sent me an interesting study on happiness involving millions of people. Did he mention it to you?

No he didn't, Grandfather. But I'd like to know what makes people happy. After all, isn't that what we're all looking for?

Well, first of all, they say that 50 percent of happiness is genetically determined. What they didn't say was that genes might act very differently in an unpolluted human being. The other 50 percent has to do with the social and psychological aspects of happiness. And if you are not genetically blessed, these aspects become, what do you say—make it or break it.

The researchers considered the usual things that Americans associate with happiness, such as money, fame, and power. But when all was said and done, happiness boiled down to four things. The first was control, being able to make choices that can change things. Second came optimism. This was discussed as being confident in what you do and being able to expect good outcomes from your endeavors. They considered religious involvement part of optimism as well. Not necessarily organized worship, but rather a sense of purpose, a sense of commitment to being part of something greater than yourself.

The third happiness factor was meaningful activity that was involving and challenging—something that brought out your gifts, so to speak. Last, and most important, were close relation-ships—those in which you felt respect and love on both sides, where giving and receiving were a joy. It turns out that the hap-piest people live in small communal settings where there is a strong sense of shared commitment to a higher ideal and the will-ingness to sacrifice for the greater good. Now when everything was tallied up, who do you think were the happiest people in the United States?

The Indians?

Sadly, Grandson, this was not true. The communities, land, work, and self-control that made our people happy were taken from us long ago. Indians live in a state of misery now, for the most part. There are pockets of traditional people left, and there is certainly a great resurgence among us, but without a fuller return to community strength, I cannot see how we will be a happy people again. This is the great challenge facing us.

It turns out that the happiest people in the country are the Amish. They are one of the few real tribal societies left fully intact in the United States. They shun most of what modern culture has to offer and what is generally considered to bring material happiness. They do not use electricity or have automobiles. They farm in the old ways, with horse and plow. When a barn needs raising, all pitch in. Their few possessions are handmade with care and pride, beautiful to behold like our own bowls, clothing, and beadwork of long ago. And their food is wholesome, nourishing, and prepared with love.

For the Amish, community comes before the individual, and all are cared for. They have no need for jails, welfare, or policemen. Nor do they have a complex bureaucracy to rule their lives. Once again they rely on the strength of their elders to keep alive the traditions and the old ways. They share what they have with each other, so that isolation and loneliness cannot take root. They are frugal and use only what they need.

Abundance, Grandson, does not mean having many possessions. It means having what you need and being able to share in the joy of life and join in a good purpose with others. Since the Amish have a set of values and beliefs to which they all adhere, they have common cause. And, most important, they are tied to the land.

The Amish people do not move about looking for new opportunities, but instead they nourish what is before them. Like the Indians of old, they are true stewards of life. I have spent some time with them, not a great deal, but enough to know that they are a joyful people. They are quiet around strangers and may even appear dour, but among their own they are a lively and celebratory people.

In the 1970s, many young people in our culture started communes because, in our hearts, Grandfather, we longed for the kind of life you describe among the Amish. But most of those communes didn't last. I've thought about why. Maybe it was because so many of the founders were depressed and angry with the larger culture. And maybe it was because a lot of them were on drugs, trying to get a spiritual high from substances instead of from the community. Some were also personality cults organized around a charismatic leader, and that usually doesn't last long because people can't find their own strength. But maybe so many failed because there weren't many elders to give guidance, nor a strong enough set of beliefs and values they could commit to.

Many of the communes were land-based, though, and committed to a simpler way of life. In the 1970s, the environmental movement took off, and people experimented with using solar power or wind energy and growing food organically. When Jimmy Carter was president, the government even gave a tax credit to people who built solar greenhouses, windmills, and other sources of clean energy. But when Reagan took office, the tax credit was taken away. I'm hoping that someday I can live in a communal setting. That's why I love your stories about the old Indian communities so much. I'd love to be a White Indian, Grandfather, and go back to those old ways you described.

Your generation is the hope for a new future, Grandson. And if you can find a way to live in harmony in smaller groups once again, with all the generations present and committed to a higher purpose, then you will be helping to bring His Crazy Horse's vision into being. I pray for this future, and for the health and happiness of your people and of all peoples of the Earth.

When you say you would like to be a White Indian, Grandson, a hundred years ago and more there were many such people who forsook the European lifestyle and settled with my people. The founder of the modern inductive and empirical scientific method was Francis Bacon. He died in 1626, and sometime before that he wrote:

> It hath often been seen that a Christian gentleman, wellborn and bred, and gently nurtured, will, of his own free will, quit his high station and luxurious world, to dwell with savages and live their lives, taking part in all their savagery. But never yet hath it been seen that a savage will, of his own free will give up his savagery, and live the life of a civilized man.

Many of the early colonists defected from colonial society to live among the Indians. Even those who had been captured often chose to remain with the tribe even when they were free to leave. You might enjoy reading the many accounts of these captives and the joy they found in their new communities, Grandson.

In his *History of the Five Nations of Canada*, published in 1747, Reverend Colden wrote:

> No Arguments, no Intreaties, nor Tears of their Friends and relations, could persuade many of them to leave their new *Indian* Friends and Acquaintance[s]; several of them that were by the Caressings of their Relations persuaded to come Home, in a little Time grew tired of our Manner of living, and ran away again to the *Indians*, and ended their Days with them. On the other Hand, *Indian* Children have been carefully educated among the *English*, cloathed [sic] and taught, yet, I think, there is not one Instance, that any of these, after they had Liberty to go among their own People, and were come to Age, would

remain with the *English*, but returned to their own Nations, and became as fond of the *Indian* Manner as those that knew nothing of a civilized Manner of living.

Before my dream under Grandfather Willow, I might have doubted those accounts, Grandfather. But I was sorry when the dream ended and I woke up. I would rather have stayed in that village and given up everything that I have, including fast food lunches and computers! In fact, sometimes I feel waves of sadness because I can't go back to that dream, to those people.

So, Grandson, you are homesick for a past that you never lived personally. And yet that past is encoded in your genes. We are children of the Earth, and she has shaped our desires and given us a blueprint for happiness. No wonder you wish to return to that blueprint, now that you have had a taste of what it feels like to live in harmonious accord with the natural world and all your relations.

Colden wrote about how White people who had lived among the Indians generally did not want to return to their culture. That same theme is repeated again and again in many other writings of the 1700s. Hector de Crevecoeur, who published a book on colonial life in 1782, summarized what we have been talking about: "Thousands of Europeans are Indians and we have no examples of even one of those Aborigines having from choice become Europeans!"

But, Grandfather. Many of the colonists lived in small communities that would have provided some of the same warmth and close relationships as Indian tribes. And they must also have had a much more comfortable standard of living in their colonial homes than in a wilderness setting. So why do you really think they stayed with people who were, essentially, kidnappers? I'd think that it would be very hard to overcome the anger and indignity of being forcibly taken from your loved ones.

That is a good question, Grandson. Perhaps it had to do with the sense of becoming fully awake and alive that the captives must have experienced among the Indians. Every human being longs to live life with passion and commitment—to put their whole body and soul into their faith and beliefs, rather than skimming the surface of things.

So while the Europeans and the Indians held many of the same spiritual and ethical values, Indian societies were far more faithful to their beliefs and principles. In John Bricknell's narrative of his capture and life among the Delaware, he wrote the following appraisal of his experience:

> The Delawares are the best people to train up children I ever was with. . . . Their leisure hours are, in a great measure, spent in training up their children to observe what they believe to be right. . . . [A]s a nation they may be considered fit examples for many of us Christians to follow. They certainly follow what they are taught to believe right more closely, and I might say more honestly, in general, than we Christians do the divine precepts of our Redeemer. . . . I know I am influenced to good, even at this day, more from what I learned among them, than what I learned among people of my own color.

There is a kind of deep excitement in feeling fully committed to anything, Grandfather. I've experienced that many times. It gives you energy, and you feel a flow of ideas and well-being. It's like all your scattered energy gets focused into a coherent beam like a laser, and you're filled with purpose and with the means to realize that purpose. One of the things that's hardest for me is boredom, which I think is the opposite of commitment. And it sounds like the Indians were very energized, very focused around their beliefs. I'll bet there was very little boredom or depression compared to our culture.

When you are attuned to the needs of others and to the wisdom of the natural world, which is always renewing and even thrilling, when you have been encouraged to find your strengths and use them, Grandson, it is very hard, indeed, for boredom to take root.

Ethnohistorian James Axtell wrote about what he called "White Indians" in colonial America and said:

> The great majority of white Indians left not explanations for their choice. Forgetting their original language and their past, they simply disappeared into their adopted society. But those captives who returned to write narratives of their experiences left several clues to the motives of those who chose to stay behind. They stayed because they found Indian life to possess a strong sense of community, abundant love, and uncommon integrity—values that the English colonists also honored, if less successfully. But Indian life was attractive for other values—for social equality, mobility, adventure, and, as two adult converts acknowledged, "the most perfect freedom, the ease of living, [and] the absence of those cares and corroding solicitudes which so often prevail with us." As we have learned recently, these were values that were not being realized in the older, increasingly crowded, fragmented, and contentious communities of the Atlantic seaboard, or even in the newer frontier settlements.

I know what the "corroding solicitudes which so often prevail with us" means to me—doing my taxes, returning phone calls from people I didn't want to talk to in the first place, paying parking tickets, being hounded by telemarketers, fighting the traffic, and generally keeping records of just about everything in life.

Although the things the White colonists were running from were somewhat different than they would be today, at the heart they were the same kinds of things. Modern culture spends so much energy in trivial, exhausting pursuits that a person often feels burned out even if they do not have to work, and there is relatively little energy left to put into relationships, which are the most important and rejuvenating parts of life.

But tribal life must have been exhausting, too, Grandfather. You told me about the incredibly long walks to move camp. Then there was the hunting, the foraging, the preserving of food. And of course, everything was handmade, and most of the materials had to be gathered.

This may seem surprising, Grandson, but the average aboriginal person works less than four hours a day. So there is plenty of time left for play, visiting, creative projects, worship, and the like. By the time the average modern person prepares for work, gets there, and returns home, at least ten hours elapse. So there is not much time for the other threads out of which the goodness of life is spun. But as I keep telling you, Grandson, the time for the old ways has passed, for the most part. The challenge is to take the best of it and find ways to create healthy, supportive community in current times. Are you at all familiar with the writings and work of the great contemporary biologist René Dubos? He had much to say about what makes people happy, creative, and healthy in community.

I've read some of his work, and I even went to a lecture that anthropologist Ashley Montague gave a few years ago, where he talked about Dubos at length. In fact, he told us that Dubos actually discovered penicillin before Fleming, but there wasn't time to tell the whole story.

Ashley Montague. Now there is a wise elder. He has shared so much about what makes societies work, and about how humans are part of the natural world rather than somewhere above and outside of it. I would have liked to hear him speak about Dubos—better still, to hear them speak to one another. There are few opportunities left to hear the wise grandfathers share their stories and experiences.

Dubos has a remarkable ability to integrate information on genetics, evolution, the environment, and social issues. Better yet, he uses his common sense to tell people what this information means to our daily lives. He is wise as well as learned, and these, Grandson, are two very separate matters. He sees through the eye of the mind, as well as through the eye of the heart. I believe he is one of the most remarkable men of our century, and a credit to your society. He has written many books, most of which I have in my library. One of my favorites is *So Human an Animal,* for which he won the Pulitzer Prize.

I have many pages of notes that I have taken over the years from his books. The study on happiness and the conclusions about the Amish brought these to mind. In a little book called *Beast or Angel?* he contends that human societies are viable only to the extent that they remain within the limits of both human nature and nature as a whole. When we step outside of those constraints, then we run into just the sort of trouble the Earth and its peoples are in today. Would you mind flipping through these notes and reading the part on tribalism aloud, Grandson, so that I can lie here on the Earth and recharge my batteries for a while?

Dubos thinks that the individuality of modern humans—I guess he's really speaking about Western culture—has degenerated into a dangerous form of egocentrism. And he speaks of the deep longing for tribal connection, citing events as different as Woodstock and the annual New Years gathering in Times Square where people wait to see the ball drop as evidence of the need to reconnect with the tribe.

He writes:

> *The real purpose of these celebrations may not be to mark a particular event or time of the year, but rather to experience—be it only for a few hours—the warmth of tribal life. The search for unity has persisted throughout the ages as if it were a fundamental need of humankind.*

He thinks we are a society in mourning for our losses. There's an interesting quote here that he got from Maxim Gorki about what we've lost:

> *This vile life, unworthy of human reason, began on that day when the first individual tore himself away from the miraculous strength of the people, from the masses, from his mother, and frightened by his isolation and his weakness, pitied himself and grew to be a futile and evil master of petty desires, a mass that called itself "I." It is this same "I" which is the worst enemy of man.*

That is a strong statement, but a good and true summary of all we have spoken about. A man away from his connections is truly a pitiful creature. He is left to glorify his fearful ego, that sense of "I" that becomes like a malignancy, running rampant through the body of society. Dubos makes the point that this sense of ego is unnatural. We did not evolve to operate this way. And I am sure you know from your studies, Grandson, that when our behavior opposes our biology, great and unnatural stress is the result.

I think I've got that part about how we evolved right here, Grandfather:

> *It was while living in tribes of hunter-gatherers and in compact villages during the millennia before and after the development of agriculture that humankind acquired certain*

social attitudes which still condition its behavior in modern societies. Since human nature has been shaped by the conditions prevailing in tribes and villages, the genetic code which governs the responses of the human brain probably became adapted to social relationships involving only limited numbers of people. A few recent observations seem to favor this.

Ah, now he gets to the Amish! He says that they have basically remained unchanged since they came to this country some three centuries ago. Their method of making communal decisions, and often even private ones, "must be taken in common by a kind of Quaker 'sense of the meeting.'" He notes that making decisions this way becomes more difficult if the group exceeds a certain size, and this would make the peace which the Amish enjoy within their communities more difficult to maintain. So when an Amish community gets up to around 500 people, it will split into two smaller groups, with the offshoot group moving to start a new community.

This is exactly what my people did. That is why there were so many bands, yet we all came together at certain times during the summer months for ceremonies, socializing, dancing, and the hope of meeting a mate from another band. That way, the entire tribe kept in close touch, and there were many stories to share each summer.

Dubos cites a study from the University of Pittsburgh that showed that people usually know only about 800 to 1,200 people "well enough to remember the first name." And then he continues:

> *But knowing the name does not necessarily mean knowing the person. More important is to recognize the voice and turns of phrase; the gestures and ways of walking; certain expressions of the lips and eyes; the habits, opinions, and familial*

antecedents. These are the kind of details that permit a real identification and also a fairly reliable expectation of what the behavior of a particular person is likely to be in a particular situation. When such criteria of personality are taken into consideration, the number of persons whom we can know is rather small—on the order of a few hundred.

That makes a lot of sense from the point of view of bands functioning best when there are no more than 500 people in the community. It also speaks to the shallowness of the ideas about creating a "global village" that Marshall McLuhan has written about. Even the term *global village* shows a lack of understanding of what a real village is. *Global* and *village* are mutually exclusive terms, Grandson.

McLuhan is talking about a valid hope, but perhaps he was mistaking abstractions for people. There is no substitute for personal interaction in creating good communities. For example, television is a kind of global community. It provides a common set of experiences for people, but they are abstract rather than personal.

I see where you're leading. Dubos talks about a college girl who wrote a book about this subject in 1973. Here's an excerpt of what he says:

> *She had watched television as a voyeur, not as a person really involved in the human pathos of world events. Learning about the world through news reports, talk shows, television broadcasts gives the artificial thrill that comes from the illusion of proximity to events without the necessity of being involved in them; it does not elicit an organic interaction and therefore gives at best a trivial quality to the experience of the global village.*

I understand her experience, Grandfather. There's a world of difference between the crime shows that I've seen on television and what it must really be like to be involved in a high-speed chase along a crowded interstate. In real life, my heart would be racing, I'd probably be hyperventilating, and I know I'd be terrified.

Exactly. So you would never want it to happen again. The trauma might ignite an urge to help or serve or change the system in some way so that all that chasing would not be necessary. A mother whose son is killed by a drunk driver will never be the same again. In fact, just such a woman organized MADD, Mothers Against Drunk Drivers. And sorry to say, it took the real experience of loss for that to happen.

Current Western society, which is a microcosm of a global village, is so large and impersonal that it is hard to care about things personally. In fact, seeing television murders, rapes, chases, and wars actually creates a kind of numbness, a dissociation from their real-life counterparts.

Television and the news commentators have sort of taken the place of elders in our society, don't you think? The storytelling is electronic, and for the most part the stories are about violence, betrayal, hatred, and disaster.

Another problem is that children watch most television alone. There is no one to discuss the stories with them who might place them in a larger context. Even when the stories told are good ones, much of their power remains untapped, for we need to understand stories in reference to our own lives and those of our loved ones. Otherwise they remain abstractions, and we are not as likely to remember them. Once again, Grandson, knowledge is of the mind and wisdom of the heart. And wisdom is embodied; it becomes part of our lived experience, and that is its power. We can and will use it to make changes in our lives and in the world.

Everything we've talked about today seems like common sense, Grandfather. I wonder how we could have forgotten the most basic need for community.

You have not forgotten it, Grandson. The same hope and desire for love, respect, and close friendships has motivated human beings from the beginning of time. If we could forget it, perhaps people would not be so anxious and depressed. For these conditions stem from grief, a deep recognition that those things most meaningful, simple, and sacred are not easily found in today's society.

I've always had a vision of forming some kind of community on my family land in Virginia, Grandfather. But today a crucial piece fell into place. Like the communes of the '70s, I envisioned a haven for people my own age. Now I know that without elders and children, people of every age, a community is not an organic whole. I've got a lot to think about. And a lot of gratitude. I know how I want to live. Now I have to find the way and become part of the solution to a problem that your people's prophecies have marked as a point of choice. Purification or resurrection, that's the fork in the road where we stand.

CHAPTER NINE

HEALING THE BODY AND THE PLANET

John and Chasing Deer packed a knapsack of water, fruit, bread, and jerky and took off through the summer woods, following the elk trail east past the pond where John had gone with Sister Fox. In spite of the old man's limp, his pace was steady and strong. After about an hour, John's hips began to ache from the uneven terrain. "Hey, Grandfather," he called, "my shock absorbers aren't as good as yours. Do you think we could stop and rest for a while?"

"It is only another two or three miles to the wildflower meadow, Grandson. Just focus your intention on the destination, and Grandmother Earth will carry you there. I want to show you the flowers when Grandfather Sun is at his highest point, and this afternoon there is going to be a thunderstorm. Maybe with hail. So we must move on in order to reach the meadow and return to the cabin before the Thunder Beings visit, unless you feel that you cannot make it without a break."

John took a deep breath and summoned his strength to continue. After all, Chasing Deer was almost a hundred years older than the young athlete. *If he can do it,* John thought, *then so can I.*

In another hour, the narrow trail opened into a mountain meadow that shone with flowers that looked like jewels strewn on a green carpet. The delicate yellow blossoms of wild peas and snapdragons formed a counterpoint to the red and orange of the Indian paintbrush. The air was filled with the fresh fragrance of big leaf sage, and clusters of purple locoweed swayed in the gentle breeze. The sky was azure, and not a cloud was in sight.

"Grandfather," John smiled with delight, "this place looks like a playground for fairies and little people. It's enchanting. I've never seen so many wildflowers before."

"Indeed you are right, Grandson. Many nature spirits live in this meadow. Let us sit down on the log by that little stream over there so that I can rest my bum leg and you can rest your two good ones." He laughed. Giving thanks to The Great Mysterious, they opened their pack and drank deeply from the sweet water from Chasing Deer's well. As they ate their simple lunch, John asked the elder how he knew that a storm was coming, since there was still not a cloud in the sky.

"When you have lived as long as I have, Grandson, you can feel the weather in your bones. Besides, Sister Fox told me this morning," he added, an impish grin crinkling up the corners of his bright eyes. As they sat together in the pristine meadow, John's heart was filled with gratitude for the beauty, but also with sadness at the thought that even here, so far from civilization, the afternoon storm would carry pollution and acid rain. It was of the health of the Earth, and of the people, that they talked that day, late into a night made fresh by a summer storm.

John: I can't believe what good shape you're in for a man of your age, or of any age for that matter, Grandfather. That was a long hike, and you don't seem the least bit tired.

Chasing Deer: Looks can deceive, Grandson. The walk was not so easy, but I am used to walking. And we did not go so far—only about nine or ten miles round trip. My people have always been hardy and fleet of foot, and even elders like me could walk many miles when moving camp. According to your records, the first sub-four-minute mile was run in 1954 by Roger Bannister. But it was really not the first on record. In 1876 the Pawnee scout *Kootah-wecoot-soole-lehoola-shar,* or Big Hawk Chief, ran a recorded sub-four-minute mile while working for the United States Army.

Ohiyesa tells of how his grandmother swam across a swift river with him on her back while in her late 60s "because she did not wish to expose me to accident in one of the clumsy round boats of bull-hide which were rigged up to cross rivers which impeded our way, especially in the springtime." He also remembers his grandmother walking "25 miles without appearing much fatigued" at the age of 82.

Ernest Thompson Seton, who you will remember was the founder of the Boy Scouts, was so impressed with the physical endurance of the Indian that he wrote several pages in his book *The Gospel of the Redman* relating feats of endurance that he had either witnessed or had read about from reliable sources. He was present when a young Cree brought in dispatches from 125 miles away in 25 hours. Seton was impressed by the fact that this was considered a normal occurrence by all present.

The Tarahumare Indians who carried mail from Chihuahua to Batopiles, Mexico, regularly ran more than 500 miles a week, and Hopi messengers were known to run 120 miles in 15 hours. From my own People, Chief Running Antelope got his name as a boy by chasing and finally catching an adult antelope in a five-hour flat-out run.

One of the reasons that the United States Army could not catch Geronimo and his band was that they could walk 70 miles a day in the rugged southwestern mountains. And our ruggedness made us hard to kill off, Grandson. The old Indian fighter, Colonel Richard Dodge, wrote:

The shock or blow of a bullet will ordinarily paralyze so many nerves and muscles of a Whiteman as to knock him down, even though not striking a vital part. The Indian gives no heed to such wounds, and to "drop him in his tracks," the bullet must reach the brain, the heart, or the spine. I have myself seen an Indian go off with two bullets through his body, within an inch or two of the spine, the only effect of which was to cause him to change his gait from a run to a dignified walk.

Keeping in shape in our culture isn't the norm, Grandfather, so it's become a whole industry. Even my mother has a personal trainer who puts her through her paces at the gym three times a week. And though she's a lot younger than Ohiyesa's mother, I'm sure she couldn't swim across a river with a young boy on her back, ducking obstacles. Anyway, in spite of all we've learned about fitness and exercise in the past ten years, people are fatter and more sedentary now than ever before. I read that 54 percent of adults and 35 percent of children are overweight.

Unfortunately, this is true of my people, also, Grandson. And our lifespan is less than half of what it was in the old days. Luther Standing Bear has spoken about the serious decline in Indian health that occurred with the coming of the White man and the disruption of our natural relationships to the Earth. He wrote, "I can remember grandfather, old when I was just a child, deploring the situation, saying there was a time in his memory when people did not speak of disease. It was not a subject of conversation, not being an experience in life of any importance."

I once made an informal study of longevity amongst several hundred Indians known in the historical records, most of whom were born before there was much contact with the White man. I found the average lifespan to be about 80, with over 20 percent living to be 100 or older. What we are told today is that the average lifespan has never been longer, due to the miracles of modern science. That may be true for those of European descent, but not for Indians.

When we go back to the cabin, look on the wall by the fireplace and you will see a picture of a group of very old Indians, though most of them do not look as old as they are. They are all Lakota warriors who fought as young men in the Battle of Greasy Grass, or Little Big Horn, as it is called. The picture was taken 72 years after the battle. I believe that old Nick Black Elk was the youngest one there, and the picture claims that he was 98.

Our people lived longer and healthier lives than people of today despite all the modern medicine available. The Europeans who first came upon the Indians often remarked on this. Amerigo Vespucci wrote in his journals, "They live one hundred and fifty years, and rarely fall ill, and if they do fall victims to any disease, they cure themselves with certain roots and herbs."

He was also impressed by the way our women retained their youthful figures. "It was to us a matter of astonishment that none was to be seen among them who had a flabby breast, and those who had borne children were not to be distinguished from virgins by the shape and shrinking of the womb." I am sure that Vespucci was inaccurate in estimating the lifespan to be 150 years, but the point is that the Indians must have been very old compared to the Europeans in his experience.

Fred Last Bull, the Keeper of the Sacred Arrows of my mother's People, the Cheyenne, wrote in 1957, "Our old food we used to eat was good. . . . Today we eat white man's food, we cannot live so long—maybe seventy, maybe eighty years, not a hundred."

And an old Micmac chief said in 1676:

> It is true that we have not always had the use of bread and of wine which your France produces; but, in fact, before the arrival of the French in these parts, did not the Gaspesians live much longer than now? And if we have not any longer among us any of those old men of one hundred and thirty to forty

years, it is only because we are gradually adopting your manner of living, for experience is making very plain that those of us live longest who, despising your bread, your wine, and your brandy, are content with their natural food of beaver, of moose, of waterfowl, and fish, in accord with the custom of our ancestors and of all the Gaspesian nation.

With poor food, the despair and resultant alcoholism, the outlawing of our religious practices, and all the other miseries, the reservation Indian now lives an average of about 40 years. Diabetes, alcoholism, heart disease, and depression have taken a terrible toll on my people, once among the healthiest on the Earth.

I'm shocked, Grandfather. Forty years is barely mid-life. What a terrible state of affairs—a total reversal of the natural order of things. Now I know why Tommy is studying to become a medicine carrier, and why he is so interested in nutrition as well. He is totally devoted to your People, and there is such a desperate need.

Perhaps, Grandson, the Purification will occur not through Earth changes or atomic destruction, but more insidiously, through an erosion of health due to lack of exercise and poor nutrition. And even those who eat a healthy diet are now consuming food that is filled with toxins because of the poisoning of the air and water resulting from industrialization and destruction of the Earth's natural ecosystems. Modern medicine has proved an excellent way to combat bacterial disease and repair grave injuries to the body, but the cancer and heart disease brought upon people through pollution, stress, and unhealthy lifestyles would be better prevented than managed by medicine. Technology is a help in some instances, yet to rely on it as a protector of health is treating the symptoms and not the underlying problem.

I was reading the rest of your notes from Dubos last night, Grandfather, and he makes the point that we can't depend on technology to save the Earth, which is exactly what most people are counting on. We've been trained to think that science can fix every problem, including the destruction of the environment. He says:

> *The problems of poverty, disease, and environmental decay cannot be solved merely by the use of more and more scientific technology. Technological fixes usually turn out to be a jumble of procedures that have unpredictable consequences and are often in conflict with natural forces. Indeed, technological magic is not much better than primitive magic in dealing with fundamental issues of human existence, and in addition, it is much more destructive.*

He goes on to say that we tend to concentrate on the degradation of the environment and the disease that it causes, but that there is still something more critical, more essential that we are overlooking.

And what might that be, Grandson?

From all we've discussed, and from the experiences I've had of the natural world, Grandfather, it's obvious that we get a lot more than food and shelter from Grandmother Earth. The connection runs much deeper. For example, as a child I was very happy that my mother was alive and well because I needed her to feed and clothe and house me or I would have died. But our relationship was much richer than that. We shared love and joy. She was a teacher and a friend. In many ways, she shaped my entire life and the evolution of who I am in terms of my values. And I think that our relationship to Grandmother Earth is a lot like that.

Grandfather Willow and Sister Fox are my teachers, as are you. Since I've been here, I've learned from the wind and the water. I can relate to Chief Seath'l when he called the rivers our brothers. Filtering out the pollutants in them so that we can drink doesn't make the rivers healthy. And if they are not, we lose something intangible but very precious.

Go back to the dream you had beneath Grandfather Willow, Grandson. You sensed your connection to the Earth so deeply that day.

Well, this is hard to put into words, but I sensed that the learning, the creativity, the love of the people in that Indian village was fed from a kind of energy emanating from the Earth. They seemed perfectly in tune with subtle signals that came from the land. It was as if the Earth provided the nourishment and the direction that their minds needed to properly develop. Sort of like a forcefield that imposed a level of organization on everything from their bodies to their thought processes. Maybe that's not so strange after all, Grandfather, since we have evolved out of the land itself. Dubos wrote about this very thing. Just give me a moment to find the place:

> *If men were to colonize the moon or Mars—even with abundant supplies of oxygen, water, and food, as well as adequate protection against heat, cold, and radiation—they would not long retain their humanness, because they would be deprived of those stimuli which only Earth can provide. Similarly, we shall progressively lose our humanness even on Earth if we continue to pour filth into the atmosphere; to befoul soil, lakes, and rivers; to disfigure landscapes with junkpiles; to destroy wild plants and animals that do not contribute to monetary values; and thus transform the globe into an environment alien to our evolutionary past. The quality of human life is inextricably interwoven with the kinds and variety of*

*stimuli man receives from the Earth and the life it harbors,
because human nature is shaped biologically and mentally by
external nature.*

*It never dawned on me that we were so dependent on
Grandmother Earth for our psychological and mental development and well-being. I'm worried that the foreign world we're
creating will spawn a different type of human being, a mutant.
And looking around at the steady increase in violence, depression, and anxiety, Grandfather, I think that's already happening.*

You sound like Frank Fools Crow, Grandson. He, too,
thought that we were becoming mutants, and I recall him saying
that it would take five full generations to return the Earth and her
creatures, including us, to a normal state. What people seem to
fear most is cancer of the body, but the mutations are also of the
soul. The challenge of the new millennium is to awaken spiritually so that we can restore our Grandmother Earth to health, for
otherwise all is lost. No amount of good-heartedness or community can prevail against a polluted world that changes our very
cells and souls.

*Most people probably have no idea of how dependent we are
on the Earth for the things Dubos talked about. And it's hard to
even get people to pay attention to basic environmental problems.
It usually goes back to jobs. I understand that problem, but it
seems like many new jobs could be created in cleaning up the
mess that's already been made.*

*The ozone layer is being eaten up. As ultraviolet rays
increase, there will be more skin cancers, cataracts, blindness,
and weaker immune systems. The excessive ultraviolet light will
also cause chemical reactions in the atmosphere that cause res-
piratory diseases. Then, of course, there is acid rain. It lowers the
pH of the soil, which kills some of the microorganisms required*

for the Earth to be fertile. It also leaches heavy metals from the ground, creating toxic water that kills animals and fish when the groundwater finds its way to the rivers. Trees die because the right nutrients aren't created anymore. That reminds me of the prophecy that the Purification will start when the elms and maples die from the top down, which acid rain is causing to happen right now.

In the early 1960s, Rachel Carson alerted the world to the danger of pesticide pollution when she wrote Silent Spring. *And I bet you know what happened, Grandfather. The chemical companies launched a vendetta against her and made her life miserable. But she was right. The damage that pesticides have caused is well documented and absolutely staggering, both in terms of physical and mental health.*

People get up in arms because tobacco companies have been hiding evidence that cigarettes were harmful for years. They should be even more outraged that chemical companies have known about the effect of pesticides like DDT for decades, and when its use was finally banned here, they just started shipping it to Third World countries. The justification for that was that it is used to spray for mosquitoes, and malaria was thought to be a greater health risk than the chemicals. But a lot of the DDT is sold to farmers for crop spraying, and then it gets shipped right back to us on all those good-looking fruits and vegetables that are out of season here, but come up from Mexico and South America.

You are quite an orator, Grandson, when you get your dander up. But that is good. It takes energy to create change and oppose a system that is so entrenched that it may literally take earthquakes to move it. There is another environmental story I would like to tell you about the food we eat. Bear with an old man as I warm up to the story with some reminiscences.

When I was a young man in my 70s, I followed football and

basketball for a few years because so many of our young people had an interest in these sports. I actually enjoyed it quite a bit, to tell you the truth. I remember that great game for the championship in 1958 between the Baltimore Colts and the New York Giants. The biggest man on the field was "Big Daddy" Lipscomb at 6'6" tall and 276 pounds. If my memory serves me right, there was only one man bigger in all of professional football. His name was Les Bingaman. He weighed about 300 pounds, but he was shorter than Lipscomb, and frankly rather fat.

Wilt Chamberlain entered professional basketball in about 1960, and it seems to me that there was only one other player seven feet tall, though I could be mistaken. Now there are seven-foot players on most every junior college team, and Lipscomb is smaller than the average major college lineman. The puzzling thing is why people are getting so big. What do you think, Grandson?

Well, people are eating much better than they used to, taking in more protein, which would account for why they're taller. And as for bulk, athletes are lifting weights and working out more, too. That probably accounts for at least some of the growth increase.

That is exactly what some scientists think. Now there were occasionally people seven feet tall or more before recent times, and I do not mean because of some hormonal disorder. Touch-the-Clouds, the great Miniconjou warrior and His Crazy Horse's uncle, was at least seven feet tall. The soldiers thought he was Goliath. But men of that size were few and far between.

And as for weight, I believe that one of the Alabama teams in the mid-'60s had a line that averaged around 210 pounds. That is not much by today's standards, although children in the '40s and '50s were much better nourished than today's children. Back then, the average middle-class family ate three square meals a day, and older children continued to drink milk like babies.

Today, families do not eat as well. Meals are taken on the go, and so much junk food is consumed. I have a theory about this. I will wager that the size increase in the past few decades is due to the growth hormones in meat and milk. These hormones may also be partially responsible for women's menses occurring years earlier than they used to and women's average brassiere cup sizes having increased almost two full sizes since World War II.

Good grief, Grandfather. I never thought we'd get around to discussing bra sizes! But that's all very interesting. I'll bet you're right. And come to think of it, I may have some other ideas about why we're becoming mutant in terms of size, and achieving more rapid sexual maturity. Cattle and chickens are sometimes fattened with estrogen as well as growth hormones. And many pesticides and pollutants have estrogenlike activity as well. These are called xenoestrogens—meaning foreign estrogens—and they get imported into our body in the fats that we eat. They're in meat, butter, eggs, vegetable oils—anywhere there's fat.

I did not know these things, Grandson. Does this mean that men will become like women, another of the old prophecies that heralds the time of the Purification?

Oh, Grandfather. I didn't even think about that. But maybe so. There was a young man a few years back who developed breasts, a condition called gynecomastia. The doctors finally figured out that his favorite food was chicken necks, and that the chickens had been implanted with estrogen pellets to make them grow faster and put on weight. When he stopped eating chicken necks, his breasts returned to normal.

But xenoestrogens may also be responsible for the prophecy that men and women are becoming the same. They have been linked to reduced penis sizes, or even missing male organs, in many animals ranging from alligators in Florida to otters in the

Columbia river in Oregon. Even if the otters still have their male parts, some of them show confused mating behavior, so their population is decreasing. Some scientists think that human beings are also being affected through reduced sperm counts, although as I recall, that is still being debated, and new research studies are being initiated.

All this debating and constantly trying to design new studies that prove there is no danger is a little bit like fiddling while Rome burns, Grandson. People will do almost anything to keep the system the way it is. But maybe in the next century we will be a race of mostly infertile giants, lonely for our children and our animal friends who will also have trouble bearing young. This brings tears to my eyes, Grandson. I can understand why Grandmother Earth, who guards our evolution, might have to take matters into her own hands and cleanse her body and ours of these poisons.

But overpopulation is a tremendous problem, too, and the biggest polluter. The Earth was not meant to harbor so many two-leggeds. Our people had very few children, both because it was better for the development of the child to have the undivided attention of its parents in the early years, and also because too many people would disrupt our relationship to Grandmother Earth. When there are too many people in any one place, like big cities, the social structure breaks down. People become strangers, and there is more crime and, of course, more pollution.

I think Dubos was correct when he wrote of pollution as a criminal act, a kind of conceit whereby we turn nature into nothing more than a source of raw materials for economic gain. He called this behavior a perversion which, if uncorrected, would kill us off. And he thought that the only salvation would be to "create a religion of nature."

Of course, the Indian has always had a religion of nature. We do not have to create one. But Dubos almost sounds like an

Indian, doesn't he? In fact, he sounds very close to Vine Deloria, who also thinks that no progress will be made in environmental law until some of our Indian "insights into the sacredness of the land derived from traditional tribal religions become basic attitudes of the larger society."

I hope that time will come to pass, Grandfather, and soon. Every time we talk, my mind goes back to the prophecies, and I see the signs pointing to the Purification more clearly. But I also know that many of my people understand the need to stem the tide of poisons and return the Earth to balance. We're also beginning to understand how important community is to health.

There was a study done years ago in the small town of Roseto, Pennsylvania. The epidemiologists were interested in this community because there was such a low level of heart disease, which is the number-one cause of death in the United States. They expected to find a health-conscious group who didn't smoke, ate low fat foods, and led an active lifestyle. To their surprise, the Rosetans' health habits were just as bad as those of most people.

What protected their health was their values and the close-knit structure of their immigrant community. People were more important than money, and the social fabric of the town was supportive and caring. But when the researchers returned 25 years later, Rosetans had been infected by the American Dream. As they began to work longer hours for more money, or move away in search of better-paying jobs, the fabric of the community weakened, and heart disease rose to the national average.

In fact, Grandfather, scientists have shown in study after study that close and loving relationships are the most important factor in health and longevity. Loneliness depresses the immune system, and cynicism and hostility make blood platelets stick to the lining of arteries and build up the plaque that leads to coronary artery disease.

This does not surprise me, Grandson. As Dubos has written, we developed genetically in tribal cultures. Our bodies are attuned to one another and to the Earth. To be healthy, we need one another and all our relations. Health and healing is in relationship—as is happiness. *Mitakuye Oyasin.*

The way to avert the Purification seems clear, Grandfather. We've got to rebuild community, care for the children and elders who ensure the Circle of Life, and restore health to the Earth. I'm leaving tomorrow, and I'm going back into a culture filled with both problems and strengths. Like Paul Ray, I think that we can take the wisdom of other cultures like yours and create a new Integral Culture like His Crazy Horse saw beneath the Great Tree of Peace. But I'm still uneasy about how that will happen. I had a dream last night, perhaps it was more than a dream, and maybe it has some part of the answer. Can I tell you about it?

Go ahead, Grandson. Dreams are often communications from the Above Beings.

I awakened in the darkness with moonlight dancing on my eyelids. The night seemed to be breathing all around me, as if all the animals and insects had synchronized into one essence. I began to breathe in rhythm with them, and a deep peace enveloped me. Whether I was asleep or awake, I did not know, but I found myself standing on top of a high mesa, moonlight illuminating the prairie that stretched endlessly below. I could see the shapes of buffalo, standing like unearthly sentries in the tall grass.

The silence of the night was suddenly broken with the flapping of enormous wings as a great horned owl swooped down. I could see its piercing yellow eyes, and its sharp talons wrapped around a stone. With a sound like thunder, the stone dropped at my feet, and the owl flew off to the west. The stone seemed to hum as if it were living, and I bent to pick up the egg-sized rock, which was made of milky white quartz, with veins of clear crystal running through it. I cupped it in my hands, and it began to emanate an aura of light in which an apparition of Sister Fox slowly took form.

"I come to bring you the blessings of Wakan Tanka," she said, not in words but in thoughts that I immediately understood.

"You are one of those that His Crazy Horse saw beneath the Great Tree of Peace, leading not only your own people, but those of the Red, Black, and Yellow races into a future of beauty. Know that the Above Beings are with you on your journey and will help you along the way. At times, their guidance will be clear. At times, you may feel as if the power has forsaken you. But that is never so. All cycles alternate between darkness and light, and in the dark times when you feel alone, the roots of new inspiration are growing beneath the soil of your conscious awareness. Trust this and give thanks to the darkness, which is the birther of life. Remember these words, little brother."

I bowed my head in thanks to Sister Fox, and then the dream faded, leaving me once again in bed, bathed in moonlight. I fell almost instantly into a deep dreamless sleep, held and rocked in what seemed like the soft womb of invisible forces. When I awakened this morning, I remembered nothing of the dream until I rolled over and found this rock, Grandfather.

Let me see it, Grandson. . . . This is truly a spirit rock, a gift from the Above Beings. It was a gift of the Owl, guardian of the night, and symbol of death and rebirth. You said that he flew away to the West. That is good, for the West is the place of change and renewal. Fresh energies move across the Medicine Wheel of the four directions from West to East. Sister Fox told you that you have been chosen as one who will help birth a new era. And she told you that you will experience times of darkness. Did you understand her words? For periods of chaos, confusion, and indecision are natural and often occur just before breakthroughs.

I know that she was preparing me for difficulties along the way, Grandfather, times when things are going badly and I might be tempted to give up, or to think that none of this had even happened.

And there will be dark times, Grandson, and times of forgetting. People think that dawnbringers are blessed with steady vision and inner peace. But that is not often so. It is more common to encounter periods of inner and outer turmoil, which like fires in the soul, refine the ore of our being. Your destiny has been offered to you as it has to each of us. But you must make the choice. Will you accept it or not? Do not speak hastily, Grandson, for you know not what you take upon yourself.

I do know that I won't be alone. The Above Beings will be there to help. And you and Tommy will, too. I trust that.

If you are ready to accept your role, Grandson, come and let us announce it to the seven circles and the two yet to come, that the sacred hoops of past and future may know that you have willingly offered yourself as a servant of life. We will make a tobacco offering to the directions, and then we will pray together with the Sacred Pipe.

I'll be leaving tomorrow, Grandfather, and I don't even have words for the gratitude I feel for all you've taught me with your humor, your sharp mind, and your good heart. But I'll admit that I am still feeling a little bit overwhelmed, trying to figure out how to help bring the wisdom of your culture into my world.

You have already expressed your gratitude, Grandson, in your attentiveness, in the wisdom you have shared with me, and in the commitment you just made to the Circle of Life. Do not struggle over trying to figure out how this new future will come or what your part will be. As each individual awakens to right relationship, the world begins to change and to offer itself newly to us. The most important thing is to have a willing heart.

The Great Mysterious leads us one step at a time, each according to his or her own gifts. Your own is the law, and you have already made the decision to use the legal system to help your Indian brothers and sisters receive what has been promised to them. Whether you succeed or fail in the cases you take on will not matter as much as your intention to help and the sacrifices you will make in so doing. Intention, as we have spoken of, is the matrix of manifestation. It creates an energy in the spirit world that calls to it the circumstances needed. This is prayer in action.

Human beings are blessed only rarely with far-seeing vision, Grandson. For the most part we see only what is before us. So when you have an intention that does not seem to come to fruition, have faith that things are working as they should be. You have put energies into motion that will work in their own time, through many people and through unforeseen circumstances. Life is like that. Most of what really happens is hidden from our view. This is why people often think that prayers are not answered. But each one is, according to a wisdom greater than our own.

Just as you found our walks in the woods easier when you gave up your anxiety about the obstacles you met along the way, and focused your heart on the beauty of the destination, so it is with bringing a new future into being. And many people, those 44 million Cultural Creatives among them, are focused on creating a new culture. There is much spirit power in that convocation of souls.

Do you know the work of the British biologist Rupert Sheldrake, Grandfather? He speaks to a change in consciousness, a new vision of a few people being able to change whole cultures. He arrived at his theories from observing the natural world of genetics and behavior. Let me give you an example. Embryos develop through what scientists call morphogenetic fields. There seems to be a kind of blueprint, or guiding force, through which an acorn becomes an oak, and an egg hatches into a bird; through which an arm becomes an arm, rather than a leg, though all the cells share the same genetic information.

We all know that there are electrical fields like the Earth's poles, and that magnets orient unfailingly to those poles. Sheldrake believes that termites build cone-shaped mounds and that wasps build their own kinds of nests in response to specific fields that produce what we think of as instinctual behavior. He calls all such organizing blueprints morphic fields, of which the morphogenetic field is a special case. He writes:

> *I suggest that the holistic, self-organizing properties of systems at all levels of complexity, from molecules to societies, depend upon such fields. Morphic fields are not fixed, but evolve. They have a kind of inbuilt memory. This memory depends on the process of morphic resonance, the influence of like upon like through space and time.*

In other words, Grandfather, we influence one another, and the evolution of a few people can affect many more. When psychologists first trained rats to run mazes, they recorded how long the training process took. When Sheldrake checked the records of different laboratories, he found that after a while, rats all over the world were learning to run mazes much faster than they had at the start. According to his theory, a kind of maze-running morphic field had been created into which the rats could tap wherever they were.

I believe that both tribal cultures and Western civilization have morphic fields, Grandfather, that have shaped our behavior. The tribal field is older, but the Western field has gained dominance. But as more and more Westerners awaken spiritually, we are beginning to resonate with the tribal field across space and time, as I did in the dream under Grandfather Willow. And I think that a new field is evolving, drawing upon what is best in the two cultures. If Sheldrake is right, it won't take too many people before that field is energized and draws others into its blueprint. What we will have then is a new dawn, the awakening of a new era.

I did not know of Sheldrake, Grandson, but his theories make sense. The fox knows where to build her den, and the geese return year after year to the same place, guided by some Mysterious Hand. For centuries people in my culture have recorded their prophecies of the time in which we now live. And there appear to be two fields of choice that they have tapped into for their information—the Purification or the Unification under The Great Tree of Peace. I hope that you are right, Grandson, and that as more and more people resonate with the vision of peace and unity, that field will draw us in and organize a harmonious return to right relationship.

Luther Standing Bear wrote:

> It is now time for a destructive order to be reversed. . . . America can be revived, rejuvenated, by recognizing a Native School of thought. . . . The old life was attuned to nature's rhythm—bound in mystical ties to the sun, moon, stars; to the waving grasses, flowing streams and whispering winds.

You have experienced those mystical ties that bind us all together, Grandson. And you have the Owl medicine stone and the help of Sister Fox to remind you of those ties in the dark and difficult times that are sure to come.

The owl's-foot necklace that I wear is many hundreds of years old. It was given to me by my great-grandfather when I was entrusted with keeping the prophecies and archives of my People. I have handed these prophecies down to you, Grandson, and the necklace, too, is now yours. Some people fear the owl. They say he is an omen of death, the power of the night. But Brother Owl is also the harbinger of change, of new winds that arise in the West and travel East. The culture of the West must now transform or perish. And you are a messenger who can help bring about good changes.

Trust always that The Great Mysterious, the force of healing, guidance, and transformation, will open the way before you as you take your place as a Keeper of Memories and walk the path of one who brings a new dawn.

Grandfather, I am without words. . . . This necklace, the owl's foot. I saw you wearing it in the Dream beneath Grandfather Willow. It was how Tommy knew that you had come to me in the dreamtime. I'll always wear it, and I'll think of you and your wisdom whenever I touch it.

I love you, Grandfather.

My days on Earth are numbered, Grandson, but we will have times together here yet. And when I have passed beyond to the Spirit World, still I will be with you.

And with that, the young White man laid his head on the shoulder of the old Indian, who stroked his silky hair in silence until the fiery disk of Grandfather Sun sank once more into the heart of the golden prairie.

NOTES

Frontispiece:

"My friend, they will return again . . ." Quoted in *The American Frontier*, ed. by Mary Ellen Jones, Greenhaven Press, San Diego, CA, p. 102.

Chapter 3:

p. 26   "the Sacred One who brought . . ." from *Voices of Earth and Sky*, Vinson Brown, Naturegraph Publishers, Happy Camp, CA, 1974, p. 70.

p. 26   The prophecies of Sweet Medicine were adapted from the version recounted in *The Cheyenne Indians*, Volume Two, George Bird Grinnell, University of Nebraska Press, Lincoln, NE, 1972, pp. 379–381 and *Cheyenne Memories*, John Stands in Timber, University of Nebraska Press, Lincoln, NE, 1972, pp. 40–41.

p. 35   "You people in the future . . ." from *The Sixth Grandfather*, edited by Raymond J. DeMallie, The University of Nebraska Press, Lincoln, NE, 1984, p. 340.

p. 36   "bearded men should come & . . ." *Beyond 1492*, James Axtell, Oxford University Press, Oxford, England, 1992, p. 34.

p. 36   "they were come to see . . ." Ibid. p. 34.

p. 36   "Men of strange appearance have come . . ." *The Invasion Within*, James Axtell, Oxford University Press, Oxford, England, 1985, p. 8.

p. 37   "It was foretold more than . . ." *Beyond 1492,* James Axtell, Oxford University Press, Oxford, England, 1992, p. 34.

p. 37   "Scattered through the world shall be . . ." Quoted in *The Discovery of America & Other Myths*, edited by Thomas Christensen and Carol Christensen, Chronicle Books, San Francisco, CA, 1992, p. 53.

p. 37   "I believe that because of these impious . . ." Ibid. p. 158.

Chapter 4:

p. 39 "I live in fear! . . ." *Words of Power,* ed. by Norbert S. Hill, Jr., Fulcrum Publishing, Golden, CO, 1994, pp. 51–52.

p. 45 "All the killers were Christian . . ." David E. Stannard, *American Holocaust,* Oxford University Press, Oxford, England, 1992, p. 153.

p. 45 "Elie Wiesel is right . . ." Ibid. p. 246.

p. 47 "They are so artless . . ." Ibid. p. 63.

p. 47 "To greet the ships with . . ." Ibid. p. 68.

p. 47 "And the people are . . ." *The Discovery of America & Other Myths,* edited by Thomas Christensen and Carol Christensen, Chronicle Books, San Francisco, CA, 1992, p. 9.

p. 48 "The houses of these Indians . . ." Ibid. p. 10.

p. 48 "We were entertained with all . . ." David E. Stannard, *American Holocaust,* Oxford University Press, Oxford, England, 1992, p. 227.

p. 49 "a race I say gentle . . ." *The Discovery of America & Other Myths,* edited by Thomas Christensen and Carol Christensen, Chronicle Books, San Francisco, CA, 1992, pp. 12–13.

p. 50 "trained in good morals." *The Invasion of America,* Francis Jennings, W.W. Norton, New York, NY, 1976, p. 5.

p. 50 "to conquer, occupy and possess . . ." Ibid. p. 5.

p. 51 "I certify to you that . . ." David E. Stannard, *American Holocaust,* Oxford University Press, Oxford, England, 1992, p. 66.

p. 52 "Tell me by what right . . ." *The Discovery of America & Other Myths,* edited by Thomas Christensen and Carol Christensen, Chronicle Books, San Francisco, CA, 1992, pp. 187–188.

p. 53 "I am recording what I have seen . . ." Ibid. p. 185.

p. 54 "tore babies from their mother's . . ." David E. Stannard, *American Holocaust,* Oxford University Press, Oxford, England, 1992, p. 72.

p. 54 "killed more than four or five million . . ." Ibid. pp. 66–80.

p. 54 "Some Christians encountered an . . ." Ibid. p. 72.

p. 55 "The Spaniards boldly entered . . ." *The Discovery of America & Other Myths,* edited by Thomas Christensen and Carol Christensen, Chronicle Books, San Francisco, CA, 1992, p. 186.

p. 55 "The Crusades had well established . . ." *The Invasion of America,* Francis Jennings, W.W. Norton, New York, 1976, p. vii.

p. 58   Chivington's men's quotes, David E. Stannard, *American Holocaust*, Oxford University Press, Oxford, England, 1992, pp. 131–133.

p. 59   "There suddenly arose such a shout . . ." Ibid. p. 134.

p. 60   "in hopes that the gospel . . ." Ibid. p. 238.

p. 61   "Civilization was the property . . ." *The Invasion of America,* Francis Jennings, W.W. Norton, New York, 1976, p. 11.

p. 61   "It pleased God . . ." David E. Stannard, *American Holocaust*, Oxford University Press, Oxford, England, 1992, p. 238.

p. 61   "for the marvelous goodness . . ." Ibid. p. 238.

p. 61   "that the Woods were . . ." Ibid. p. 238.

p. 61   "Once you have got the Track . . ." Ibid. p. 238.

p. 61   "The dogs would be an extreme . . ." Ibid. p. 241.

p. 61   "if the Indians were as . . ." Ibid. p. 241.

p. 62   "In time, a combination plan of . . ." Ibid. pp. 107–108.

p. 62   "the Principall Ende of this . . ." *The Invasion of America,* Francis Jennings, W.W. Norton, New York, 1976, p. 230.

p. 62   "there hath not been . . ." Ibid. p. 230.

p. 63   "that no Indian shall . . ." Ibid. p. 241.

p. 64   "that the Lord God . . ." Ibid. p. 183.

p. 64   "God laughed his Enemies . . ." David E. Stannard, *American Holocaust*, Oxford University Press, Oxford, England, 1992, pp. 113–114.

p. 64   "we had sufficient light . . ." Ibid. p. 114.

p. 64   "Are not the English of this land . . ." *The Invasion of America,* Francis Jennings, W.W. Norton, New York, 1976, pp. 183–184.

p. 66   "The immediate objects are the total . . ." *From the Heart,* Lee Miller, ed., Alfred A. Knopf, New York, NY, 1995, p. 105.

p. 66   "I will try to inoculate . . ." Ibid. p. 95.

p. 67   "if ever we are constrained to lift . . ." David E. Stannard, *American Holocaust*, Oxford University Press, Oxford, England, 1992, p. 120.

p. 67   "You remind me, brother, of what . . ." *Facing West,* Richard Drinnon, University of Oklahoma Press, Norman, OK, 1997, p. 86.

p. 68   "I tremble for my country . . ." *From the Heart,* Lee Miller, ed., Alfred A. Knopf, New York, NY, 1995, p. 130.

p. 68   "I have on all occasions . . ." David E. Stannard, *American*

Holocaust, Oxford University Press, Oxford, England, 1992, p. 121.

    p. 69   "The hand of heaven . . ." *Facing West,* Richard Drinnon, University of Oklahoma Press, Norman, OK, 1997, p. 108.

    p. 69   "I don't go so far as . . ." David E. Stannard, *American Holocaust*, Oxford University Press, Oxford, England, 1992, p. 143.

    p. 70   "Indian children face . . ." *Our Brother's Keeper: The Indian in White America*, Edgar Kahn, New Community Press, New York, NY, 1969, p. 64.

    p. 72   "would uncover an . . ." *Blood of the Land,* Rex Weyler, New Society Publishers, Philadelphia, PA, 1992, pp. 166–167.

    p. 72   "the main thrust of . . ." Removing children: The Destruction of Native American Families, William Byler, *Civil Rights Digest* 9 Summer, 1970, p. 25.

    p. 73   "Through the pervasiveness . . ." *Our Brother's Keeper,* ed. by Edgar S. Cahn, New Community Press, New York, NY, 1969, p. 13.

    p. 73   "he was going to kill . . ." Peter Matthiessen, *In the Spirit of Crazy Horse*, Viking Press, New York, NY, 1983, p. 62.

    p. 76   "It was a different matter . . ." *The Missionaries,* Norman Lewis, McGraw-Hill, New York, NY, 1988, pp. 96–97.

    p. 77   "Rich landowners of the municipality . . ." Ibid. pp. 98–99.

Chapter 5:

    p. 82   "In the year of 1871 . . ." This account of His Crazy Horse's prophecy was adapted from *Great Upon The Mountain,* Vinson Brown, MacMillan, New York, NY, p. 197. It was told to Brown by Chief Frank Fools Crow of the Lakota Nation.

    p. 85   "It rather represented a . . ." *The Wolves of Heaven,* Karl H. Schleiser, The University of Oklahoma Press, Norman, OK, 1993, p. 13.

    p. 86   "Be humble as the Earth . . ." *Voices of Earth and Sky*, Vinson Brown, Naturegraph Publishers, Happy Camp, CA, 1974, p. 104.

    p. 90   "with the branches full . . ." Ibid. p. 113.

    p. 94   "There are two things . . ." *Profiles in Wisdom,* Steven McFadden, Bear & Co., Santa Fe, NM, 1991, pp. 96–97.

    p. 96   "The fourth prophet told of . . ." Ibid. p. 42.

    p. 97   "When the Sixth Fire came . . ." Ibid. p. 44.

p. 97   "a little boy would . . ." Ibid. p. 44.

p. 98   "the water drum . . ." Ibid. p. 45.

p. 98   "The Creator will not answer . . ." Ibid. p. 46.

p. 100 "The major damage of television . . ." *Evolution's End,* Joseph Chilton Pearce, Harper Collins, New York, NY, 1992, p. 164.

p. 103 "It has been brought to . . ." *From a Native Son,* Ward Churchill, South End Press, Boston, MA, 1996, pp. 362–363.

p. 104 "We concern ourselves only . . ." Ibid. p. 363.

p. 105 "Many years ago when . . ." *The Zunis: Self Portrayals,* the Zuni People, University of New Mexico Press, Albuquerque, NM, 1972, quoted in *Native American Testimony*, ed. by Peter Nabokov, Penguin Books, New York, NY, 1978, pp. 439–440.

p. 109 "With this holy pipe . . ." *Seeing the White Buffalo,* Robert B. Pickering, Denver Museum of Natural History Press, Denver, CO, 1997, p. 18.

p. 111 "Now we are in a critical . . ." quoted in *Sacred History and Earth Prophecies,* Dinawa, In Print Publishing, Sedona, AZ, 1997, p. 199.

Chapter 6:

p. 119 "There are . . . many other entities . . ." *God Is Red,* Vine Deloria, Jr., Fulcrum Press, Golden, CO, 1994, pp. 152–153.

p. 119 "You ask us to think . . ." *Touch the Earth,* T. C. McLuhan, Simon and Schuster, New York, NY, 1971, p. 28.

p. 120 ". . . the women made a formal . . ." *Native American Testimony,* Peter Nabokov, ed., Penguin Books, New York, NY, 1978, p. 151.

p. 120 "Every part of all . . ." *Native American Wisdom,* Kent Nerburn and Louise Mengelkoch, eds., New World Library, Novato, CA, 1991, p. 89.

p. 120 "There is a hue . . ." *Words of Power,* Norbert S. Hill, Jr., ed., Fulcrum Publishing, Golden, CO, 1994, p. 26.

p. 129 "few people are so . . ." *The Missionaries,* Norman Lewis, McGraw-Hill, New York, NY, 1988, p. 101.

p. 129 "A primitive people is . . ." Ibid. p. 101.

p. 130 "We are related . . ." Norbert S. Hill, Jr. ed., Fulcrum Publishing, Golden, CO, 1994, p. 33.

p. 130 "Peace . . . comes within . . ." Ibid. p. 7.

p. 130 "The relationships that serve to . . ." *God Is Red,* Vine Deloria, Jr., Fulcrum Press, Golden, CO, 1994, p. 88.

p. 133 "Our religion is the tradition . . ." *The Wisdom of the Great Chiefs,* Kent Nerburn, ed., New World Library, San Raphael, CA, 1994, p. 73.

p. 134 "If any man do anything . . ." *The Gospel of the Redman,* Ernest Thompson Seton, Seton Village, Santa Fe, NM, 1963, p. 89.

p. 137 "For a Western educated . . ." *Words of Power,* Norbert S. Hill, Jr., ed., Fulcrum Publishing, Golden, CO, 1994, p. 26.

p. 138 "We saw the Great Spirit's . . ." *God Is Red,* Vine Deloria, Jr., Fulcrum Press, Golden, CO, 1994, p. 9.

p. 139 "Religion dominates the . . ." Ibid. p. 194.

p. 139 "Political activity and . . ." Ibid. p. 194.

p. 142 "did not unduly burden . . ." Ibid. pp. 269–270.

p. 143 "a true Church of God . . ." *The Gospel of the Redman,* Ernest Thompson Seton, Seton Village, Santa Fe, NM, 1963, pp. 37–38.

p. 143 "I realized that the Sioux . . . " Ibid. p. 38.

p. 144 "I tell you I never . . ." Ibid. p. 3.

Chapter 7:

p. 152 "You take something of . . ." *Words of Power,* Norbert S. Hill, Jr. ed., Fulcrum Publishing, Golden, CO, 1994, p. 37.

p. 153 "Try to do something for . . ." *Native American Wisdom,* Kent Nerburn and Louise Mengelkoch, eds., New World Library, Novato, CA, 1991, p. 33.

p. 154 "Her attitude and secret . . ." *The Soul of an Indian,* Ohiyesa (Charles A. Eastman), Kent Nerburn, ed., New World Library, San Raphael, CA, 1993, pp. 16–17.

p. 155 "They are accouched with . . ." *The Native American People of the East,* James Axtell, ed., Pendulum Press, West Haven, CT, 1973, p. 19.

p. 156 "the first and foremost cause . . ." *Evolution's End,* Joseph Chilton Pearce, Harper Collins, New York, NY, 1992, p. 126.

p. 157 "Mothers should breast feed . . ." British Medical Journal, vol. 315, December 6, 1997, p. 1487.

p. 161 "Little children were taught . . ." *Land of the Spotted Eagle,* Luther Standing Bear, University of Nebraska Press, Lincoln,

NE, 1933, pp. 15–16.

p. 162 "It was a law with . . ." Ibid. p. 2.

p. 162 "And so the days . . ." Ibid. p. 7.

p. 163 "One cannot express the . . ." *The Native American People Of The East,* James Axtell, Pendulum Press, West Haven, CT, 1973, p. 20.

p. 163 "Love of their . . ." *The Gospel of the Redman,* Ernest Thompson Seton, Seton Village, Santa Fe, NM, 1963, p. 33.

p. 163 "If you do bad . . ." *Catch the Whisper of the Wind,* Cheewa James, Horizon 2000, Sacramento, CA, 1993, p. 27.

p. 165 "Today mother-power is weak . . ." *Land of the Spotted Eagle,* Luther Standing Bear, University of Nebraska Press, Lincoln, NE, 1933, p. 109.

p. 166 "The honor of the people . . ." *Words of Power,* Norbert S. Hill, Jr., ed., Fulcrum Publishing, Golden, CO, 1994, p. 16.

Chapter 8:

p. 170 "Parental devotion was very . . ." *Land of the Spotted Eagle,* Luther Standing Bear, University of Nebraska Press, Lincoln, NE, 1933, p. 81.

p. 172 "Not a step in the . . ." *The Soul of an Indian,* Ohiyesa (Charles A. Eastman), Kent Nerburn, ed., New World Library, San Raphael, CA, 1993, p. 21.

p. 176 "It hath often been . . ." *The Gospel of the Redman,* Ernest Thompson Seton, Seton Village, Santa Fe, NM, 1963, p. xvi.

p. 176 "No Arguments, no Intreaties . . ." *The History of the Five Indian Nations of Canada,* Cadwallader Colden, London, England, 1747, pp. 203–204.

p. 177 "Thousands of Europeans are . . ." *Letters from an American Farmer,* J. Hector St. John de Crevecoeur, 1782, London, England, 1912, p. 215.

p. 178 "The Delawares are the best . . ." Narrative of John Bricknell's Captivity Among the Delaware Indians, *American Pioneer,* Vol. 1, 1842, p. 46.

p. 179 "The great majority of white . . ." *The European and the Indian,* James Axtell, Oxford University Press, Oxford, England, 1981, p. 206.

p. 182 "The real purpose of these . . . " *Beast or Angel,* René

Dubos, Charles Scribner's and Sons, New York, NY, 1971, p. 57.
    p. 182 "This vile life, unworthy . . ." Ibid. p. 216.
    p. 183 "But knowing the name . . ." Ibid. p. 85.
    p. 184 "She had watched . . ." Ibid. p. 84.

Chapter 9:

    p. 189 "because she did not . . ." *Indian Boyhood,* Ohiyesa
(Charles A. Eastman), University of Nebraska Press, Lincoln, NE,
1991, p. 26.
    p. 190 "The shock or blow . . ." *Our Wild Indians,* Richard I.
Dodge, Corner House Publishers, Williamstown, MA, 1978, p. 440.
    p. 190 "I can remember grandfather . . ." Luther Standing Bear,
University of Nebraska Press, Lincoln, NE, 1933, pp. 60–61.
    p. 191 "They live one hundred . . ." *Vespucci: Reprints, Text, and
Studies,* Vol. 5, translated by George T. Northrup, Princeton University
Press, Princeton, NJ, 1916.
    p. 191 "Our old food we used . . ." *Cheyenne Memories*, John
Stands In Timber, University of Nebraska Press, Lincoln, NE, 1972,
pp. vii–viii.
    p. 191 "It is true that we . . ." *Touch the Earth,* T. C. McLuhan,
Simon and Schuster, New York, NY, 1971, p. 49.
    p. 193 "The problems of poverty . . ." *A God Within,* René
Dubos, Charles Scribner's and Sons, New York, NY, 1972, p. 41.
    p. 194 "If men were to colonize the . . ." Ibid. p. 38.
    p. 205 "I suggest that the . . ." *Seven Experiments That Could
Change the World,* Rupert Sheldrake, Fourth Estate, London, England,
1994, p. 77.
    p. 206 "It is now time for . . ." *Land of the Spotted Eagle,* Luther
Standing Bear, University of Nebraska Press, Lincoln, NE, 1933, p.
255.

ABOUT THE AUTHOR

Kurt **Kaltreider, Ph.D.,** is of Nanticoke, German, and English descent. He graduated from Gettysburg College and holds an M.A. and Ph.D. in philosophy and clinical psychology from the University of Tennessee. Kaltreider is a leading authority on mathematical value theory, or formal axiology, upon which he based a highly successful investment model, which he uses to explore human values. Due to the erosion of traditional Indian cultures, he devotes himself full time to the protection and support of the ways of his ancestors.

Kaltreider is also the author of *American Indian Cultural Heroes and Teaching Tales.*

We hope you enjoyed this Hay House book.
If you would like to receive a free catalog featuring additional
Hay House books and products, or if you would like
information about the Hay Foundation, please contact:

Hay House, Inc.
P.O. Box 5100
Carlsbad, CA 92018-5100

(760) 431-7695 or **(800) 654-5126**
(760) 431-6948 (fax) or **(800) 650-5115 (fax)**
www.hayhouse.com

Published and distributed in Australia by:
Hay House Australia Pty. Ltd. • 18/36 Ralph St. • Alexandria NSW
2015 • *Phone:* 612-9669-4299 • *Fax:* 612-9669-4144
www.hayhouse.com.au

Published and distributed in the United Kingdom by:
Hay House UK, Ltd. • Unit 62, Canalot Studios • 222 Kensal Rd.,
London W10 5BN • *Phone:* 44-20-8962-1230 • *Fax:* 44-20-8962-1239
www.hayhouse.co.uk

Published and distributed in the Republic of South Africa by:
Hay House SA (Pty), Ltd., P.O. Box 990, Witkoppen 2068
Phone/Fax: 2711-7012233 • orders@psdprom.co.za

Distributed in Canada by:
Raincoast • 9050 Shaughnessy St., Vancouver, B.C. V6P 6E5
Phone: (604) 323-7100 • *Fax:* (604) 323-2600